District Financial Leadership Today

District Financial Leadership Today

Educational Excellence Tomorrow

Stephen V. Coffin and Bruce S. Cooper

ROWMAN & LITTLEFIELD
Lanham • Boulder • New York • London

Published by Rowman & Littlefield
A wholly owned subsidiary of The Rowman & Littlefield Publishing Group, Inc.
4501 Forbes Boulevard, Suite 200, Lanham, Maryland 20706
www.rowman.com
Unit A, Whitacre Mews, 26–34 Stannary Street, London SE11 4AB

Copyright © 2018 by Stephen V. Coffin and Bruce S. Cooper

All rights reserved. No part of this book may be reproduced in any form or by any electronic or mechanical means, including information storage and retrieval systems, without written permission from the publisher, except by a reviewer who may quote passages in a review.

British Library Cataloguing in Publication Information Available

ISBN: HB 978-1-4758-3490-1
        PB 978-1-4758-3491-8

Library of Congress Cataloging-in-Publication Data Is Available

ISBN 978-1-4758-3490-1 (cloth)
ISBN 978-1-4758-3491-8 (pbk.)
ISBN 978-1-4758-3492-5 (electronic)

Contents

Foreword *Philip H. Nisonoff*		vii
Introduction to School District Financial Leadership		ix
1	"N.A.P.E.R.R.": Steps in a Budgeting Process and Model	1
2	Enrollment Projections: Students Drive the "Budget Bus" *William Hartman and Robert Schoch*	5
3	Personnel: Education Is a People Enterprise	15
4	Special Education: Special Program Needs Budgeting	23
5	State Education Aid: How to Budget and Manage State Funding	27
6	Budgeting and Managing Federal Aid for Schools	39
7	Budgeting and Managing Local Revenues	55
8	Movements to Privatize District Funding in the United States and the United Kingdom	65
9	Managing School Districts' Funding Programs Now: Quality Education for All	69
About the Authors		77

Foreword

Philip H. Nisonoff, EdD

District Financial Leadership Today: Educational Excellence Tomorrow by Stephen V. Coffin and Bruce S. Cooper organizes and contextualizes the broad field of modern education finance at the district level to provide a practical understanding for those new to school and school district administration. Never in history has the need for district administrators skilled in school finance become so acute.

Since the U.S. economic collapse in 2008, schools have experienced reductions in funding, increased public scrutiny, calls for greater accountability systems, diversions of public funds to private and for-profit institutions, and exponential increases in employee benefit (health and retirement) costs. Simultaneously, the educational challenges have become daunting.

New curriculum standards have been advanced that call for schools to make herculean efforts above what was taught only a few years ago. Schools are being asked to educate a generation of students who have been raised on technology and media access in a system that mirrors its original design from the 1800s. The needs of serving special education students continue to grow as children are entering our school systems with diverse issues and degrees of severity unlike any time in history.

An entire legal and advocacy field in education has been established, arming parents with sufficient resources with the ability to hold school systems hostage to their demands, regardless of cost or benefit. Compensation for teachers has often not kept pace with increased costs of college tuition. Our new teachers—responsible for the future of our nation—are being asked to work for wages and benefits that barely cover the costs of their student loans and car payments. Even the security of their future is eroded as politicians have squandered their pension funds almost to brink of insolvency.

How do we manage all of this as educators? We start here. The authors and editors of this book attempt to provide a broad understanding of the educational finance system from the school district perspectives. Future administrators will benefit from gaining an understanding of how schools are funded and where the money comes from. While variations of finance systems exist across state and district levels, most principles, concepts, and vocabulary are universal and explained in detail in this work.

How do we count students? How do we plan for special education programs? How should we approach budgeting for our schools? All questions that can be answered by first obtaining a foundational understating of these concepts by reading this expertly crafted manual of education finance.

Philip H. Nisonoff, EdD
Assistant Superintendent/Business Administrator/Board Secretary,
Emerson Public Schools, Emerson, New Jersey

Introduction to School District Financial Leadership

This chapter introduces the theme of this book: that financial leadership and quality start at the district level, since funding most often comes to the district leadership, including the school board, superintendent, and financial management staff.

Thus, the central office leadership and district's school board are critical in American education, as the board, superintendent, and staff set the school district's goals, budgets, staffing, programs, and assessments for their schools. Districts are in control, and this book examines their role in improving our schools for our children—based on the school board's financial control. As such, funding and fiscal decisions must be made with systematically (carefully) and systemically, for the entire school enterprise, school by school.

We know that the school boards are usually elected locally, and often hire and fire their superintendent of schools, and, importantly, bargain collectively with the local district teachers' unions, and work to decide district spending goals, schemes, job selections, and school district standards and reviews. As one description goes:

> Most school boards have the responsibility to:
>
> 1. Establish procedures and policies for the administration of educational services in the district.
> 2. Implement the state's education laws and programs.
> 3. Monitor the operation of the school district and its programs.
> 4. Hire the district superintendent.
> 5. Oversee the annual budget preparation and resource deployment.
> —Catherine Freemans, 2002, *School Boards and Local Control: Roles and Responsibilities*

And we now see school boards under fire, as Freemans further explains,

> Currently, an increasing number of communities are rethinking ways in which to govern their local schools. Some communities have abolished local school boards altogether, while others have changed from boards appointed by state or local officials to elected boards. Some states have centralized public education governance, relieving local systems of much while others have created and greatly empowered local school councils in an effort to decentralize.

This book is the second of our two books on school finance in the United States, focusing primarily on financial leadership at the *school district* level. Our first book concentrated mainly on school-building leaders, but leading a district's finances and financial decision-making are also quite different and important for the United States has just over 13,000 separate public school districts (or LEAs, local education authorities) in the fifteen states and the District of Columbia—and thus we have many different financial policies and programs. As the Augenblick, Palaich and Associates' (APA; 2016) study examined the following:

> First, APA reviewed the revenues and expenditures of districts meeting specific performance standards. The review included an examination of base expenditures (expenditures regardless of student need) and expenditures for the students with special needs, including economically disadvantaged students, English Language Leaner (ELL) students, and special education students.
>
> Second, APA examined the differences in non-instructional spending across regions of the state. Cost areas to be included in this examination (as required by the RFP) were food service, transportation, maintenance and operations (M&O), community service, and adult education. The RFP also required an examination of the differences in revenues available to school districts by region and the differences in district expenditures by area.

We know that these some 13,500 public school districts in the United States are very different in location, size, demography, financing, taxation, wealth, needs, and quality. And some states have witnessed "equity lawsuits," where individuals and groups brought court actions to press for greater equity for the states' school districts. Hawaii is the only state with no local school districts, with the whole state and islands run by one superintendent, school board, and budget.

Thus, school finance is greatly influenced—and differs—district by district, state by state, and eventually school by school. And this book also explains and explores the financial legal actions, beginning in the early 1970s in California. For while the *Brown* decision declared racial segregation illegal in schools and classrooms, *Serrano v. Priest* (1971, 1976) stated that states cannot allow children to be given a poor education because of low local property and citizens' wealth of their home school district. The cases are much like the *Brown* desegregation case in revolutionizing the funding of public schools.

The cases are as follows.

SERRANO I (1971)

Initiated in 1968 in the Superior Court of Los Angeles County, *Serrano v. Priest* (John Serrano was a parent of one of several Los Angeles public school students; Ivy Baker Priest was the California state treasurer at the time and former U.S. treasurer) set forth two causes of action (quotes from the decision).

1. "[As] a direct result of the financing scheme they are required to pay a higher tax rate than [taxpayers] in many other school districts in order to obtain for their children the same or lesser educational opportunities afforded children in those other districts."
2. "[That] an actual controversy has arisen and now exists between the parties as to the validity and constitutionality of the financing scheme under the Fourteenth Amendment of the United States Constitution and under the California Constitution."

SERRANO II (1976) OR *RODRIGUEZ*

In *San Antonio Independent School District v. Rodriguez* (1973), the Supreme Court of the United States reversed a similar decision by a Texas District Court, which like *Serrano I* had been decided on Fourteenth Amendment equal protection grounds. In *Serrano I*, however, the California Supreme Court had relied in addition on California's constitution, and in *Serrano II* it affirmed that basis, protecting the *Serrano* decisions from *Rodriguez*.

The *Serrano II* decision also held that the legislative response to *Serrano I* was insufficient and affirmed the trial court's order requiring that wealth-based funding disparities between districts be reduced to less than $100 per child by 1980.

Five years after the first *Serrano* decision in California, the same issues arose in the public schools of San Antonio, Texas, and the U.S. High Court—in what became *Serrano* II (1976)—ruled that *Serrano I* struck down California's public school, general-fund, financing structure as a violation of equal protection because under this system, per-pupil expenditures varied greatly and depended on a school district's tax base. These kinds of tax-base disparities resulted in inequalities in actual educational expenditures per pupil that the state-aid mechanisms—designed to ensure a minimum "foundation" level of expenditure—were wholly inadequate to offset. See more at http://corporate.findlaw.com/law-library/separate-and-unequal-serrano-played-an-important-role-in.html#sthash.

SERRANO III (1977)

Serrano III dealt primarily with attorneys' fees but in passing affirmed the trial court's response to the *Serrano II* decision, including a six-year timetable for bringing the funding system into compliance.

Thus, the field of school finance moved toward greater equity that requires school district leaders to understand the law and court decisions in their state. Other roles for the school district leaders include the following: (1) policy-setting for the district that will be implemented in each school; (2) personnel decisions, such as the hiring (and firing)s of principals and assistants; (3) funding of teacher lines in each school that is often made in the district office; and (4) handling and bargaining with the district's unions—teachers, principals, assistant principals, guidance personnel.

Financial decisions of the superintendents and other officers affect the personnel and operations of the individual schools and classrooms. This book, thus, builds the framework—financial, operational, and policy-based—for schools overall, although principals and staff have an important impact on teaching and learning in each school.

CONCLUSION

Thus, sound *district* finances and management are integral to the provision of a quality education. Indeed, a school district's budget is the financial representation of its educational plan. Thus, a clarion alert for all teachers: "If it's not in your budget, it won't be in your classroom for your students."

However, sound district finance is increasingly challenging in an era of scarce resources and increasing pressure on schools and districts to improve. Therefore, this book provides an in-depth understanding of fundamental practices, processes, and lessons learned that not only will benefit all school administrators, personnel, parents, students, and other stakeholders but also undergird the provision of an excellent education.

This book will focus on key building blocks essential for the provision of an excellent education. The value proposition inherent in this book should work well for all schools, districts, students, and school stakeholders, regardless of location, type, and demographic mix. The components of sound district finance and management—that are increasingly important in an era of scarce financial, material, and human resources—are provided in this book, along with some clear and related recommendations.

Three recommendations are important in this chapter. First, be aware that most changes and innovations in education have associated costs; second, *leaders should investigate these expenses, often related to personnel salaries*; and third, leaders should *present and support the potential costs into the future*.

REFERENCES

Augenblick, Palaich and Associates (2016). *School finance*. (Online)
Freemans, C. (2002). *School boards and local control: Roles and responsibilities*. Georgia State University; Andrew Young School of Policy Studies.

Chapter 1

"N.A.P.E.R.R."

Steps in a Budgeting Process and Model

INTRODUCTION

This chapter describes and analyzes the critical steps in school district financial leadership, for school superintendents and principals are critical leaders in finding, organizing, and using education resources in their schools to meet the various needs of their students and staff. Budgeting—as a process—is critical in almost every effort, and learning to budget—the process and the products—is also all important. This chapter presents a tried-and-true process for successful, adaptive budgeting for programs in schools. We have crafted a six-step process, called N.A.P.E.R.R., to make this happen, and we show how, when, and why. First, let's define the six-step process:

First: "N" = NEEDS: Develop and explain all *needs* by asking the stakeholders what they want and require to improve their program or classrooms, and then compile needs without any specific order. Making sure all stakeholders are represented is central to developing a consensus and support for the effort. Districts increasingly are involving teachers in the process. School business administrators (SBAs) should ask principals to question supervisors or departmental heads and, then, to ask their teachers what they believe their educational needs are.

Teachers should identify needs such as classroom furniture, ceiling, window, heating, electrical, water if applicable, supplies, materials, computers or computer time, whiteboards, books, paper goods, manipulative and other classroom items, but not salary or benefit items that are controlled centrally.

Second: "A" = ASSUMPTIONS: Have each stakeholder and budget person develop an undergirding set of *assumptions and arguments* for each item in the proposed budget. Providing assumptions to support each identified need is essential. Assumptions address the key "why is this needed?" question and help in decision-making! Stakeholders must keep in mind that their assumptions may not be and are not always obvious to those who will use their input to make final budgetary decisions! Assumptions help to support the level of need and justify the costs and efforts.

Third: "P" = PRIORITIES: Prioritize all NEEDS, based on their assumptions and implied importance. Teachers should and can prioritize their needs before submitting them to their supervisors or department heads—which in turn would lead to their particular needs, assumptions, prioritization, and rationale before submitting them to their principal and the superintendent and school board. In turn, the principal adds his or her needs, assumptions, prioritization, and rationale to the document including his or her overview of his or her school's needs, assumptions, prioritization, and rationale.

Fourth: "E" = EXPENDITURES: How to organize to make it happen, based on finance availability and *expenditures*? Without adequate funding, the program will have difficulty operating and growing. How to get organized and staffed in schools to make the budget work real and effective?

Fifth and Sixth: Double-"R" = RATIONALE and REVIEW: And finally, how to provide a *rationale* and *review* process for each priority, per item, will help justify and improve its relative importance in the budget, and how the program or other budget uses may be reviewed and evaluated at some point. Each level of the process should provide a rationale, starting with the teachers. (N.A.P.E.R.R. should be truly based on teachers' inputs and school and classroom collective needs.)

Once N.A.P.E.R.R. is completed—with all stakeholders active in the process—the leaders must see if anyone receives cuts to aid or meet sudden increased costs. If this results in a budget gap, teachers and school-building leaders can quickly contact each provider of that item, reassess its priority, and make selective rather applying across-the-board percentage cuts (unsound and usually backfire).

Projected program and service offerings can and often do change during the process, making budgeting a dynamic process; however, at a certain point having done the best possible effort, the budget is submitted for BOE approval or central office approval if it is a private or charter school, which often includes board of governors/trustees' approval.

N.A.P.E.R.R. can be used in districts and schools to help develop budgets, large or small, in both the public and private sectors. Students and others have successfully used N.A.P.E.R.R. in job interviews and in their careers. N.A.P.E.R.R. provides a sound conceptual and practical framework for budgeting.

The first step in developing a budget for a school is to determine the *needs*. As Edwards, Ezzamel, McLean, and Robson (2000) explain, the budget determination is a two-step process, as follows:

> First to satisfy their statutory duties LEAs supervised the introduction of internal systems of budgetary control and school development planning in schools. Thus, control procedures were largely designed by internal auditors, who sought to provide an audit trail and to ensure financial probity mainly to satisfy external legitimacy, rather than to influence internal decision-making.
>
> Second, the specific nature of the relationship between budgeting and strategy varies between schools, as the extent of formalized planning differs; but in general there is a very loose coupling between strategic objectives and budget expenditures. (pp. 1–2)

CONCLUSION

The recommendations come clearly from this chapter's N.A.P.E.R.R.: step by step, since most—if not all—schools in their school districts, first, have the N—*needs*, the steps are to set priorities, share them, and make a case for funding and meeting the needs. The recommendations are as follows:

> Second, N.A.P.E.R.R. allows leaders to follow the second step, the *assumptions"*, in setting and gaining the funds, at the school and classroom levels, to make the goals work—all steps are essential to the improve uses of funding, now and in the future.

This model both clarifies and simplifies the complexities of school district financial leadership. Following N.A.P.E.R.R., leaders at the school district level can conceptualize and begin to analyze the finances of their school district—a key goal of this book.

Thus, our recommendations are that each school leader should adopt a form of N.A.P.E.R.R., or at least the main parts, to assist in making quality decisions. In a few sentences, district leaders need to assess the programs and problems with assumptions.

REFERENCE

Edwards, P., Ezzamel, M., McLean, C., & Robson, K. (2000). Budgeting and strategy in schools: The elusive link. *Financial Accountability & Management, 16*(4), 21–36.

Chapter 2

Enrollment Projections

Students Drive the "Budget Bus"

William Hartman and Robert Schoch

INTRODUCTION

Projections of student enrollments provide the baseline estimates of the level of district operations *and expenditures* for the upcoming year. As such, these data represent the initial step in preparing the district's budget. Accurate projections are essential since they determine or influence many of financial estimates that go into the budget, particularly in the instructional area. Thus, this chapter analyzes the key variables in financial budgeting and projections, including enrollment, by grade level, goals, and children's talents and educational, emotional, and physical needs.

Figure 2.1 illustrates the major connections that link student projections to district operations and budget estimates; practically all of the important areas of school and district level activities are included. This chapter puts student enrollments, grade levels, and needs and spending on the same page, as is essential in many school district finances—"program costs per pupil."

- Personnel. Accurate student enrollment projections are critical for the personnel components of the budget since salaries and benefits costs—for district staff demands, based on enrollment—represent the largest expenditure areas in a school district. On the one hand, getting both the appropriate number and qualifications of staff to meet the educational needs of students is vital to providing an effective education. On the other hand, the educational needs must be balanced with the fiscal and political constraints that the district faces.

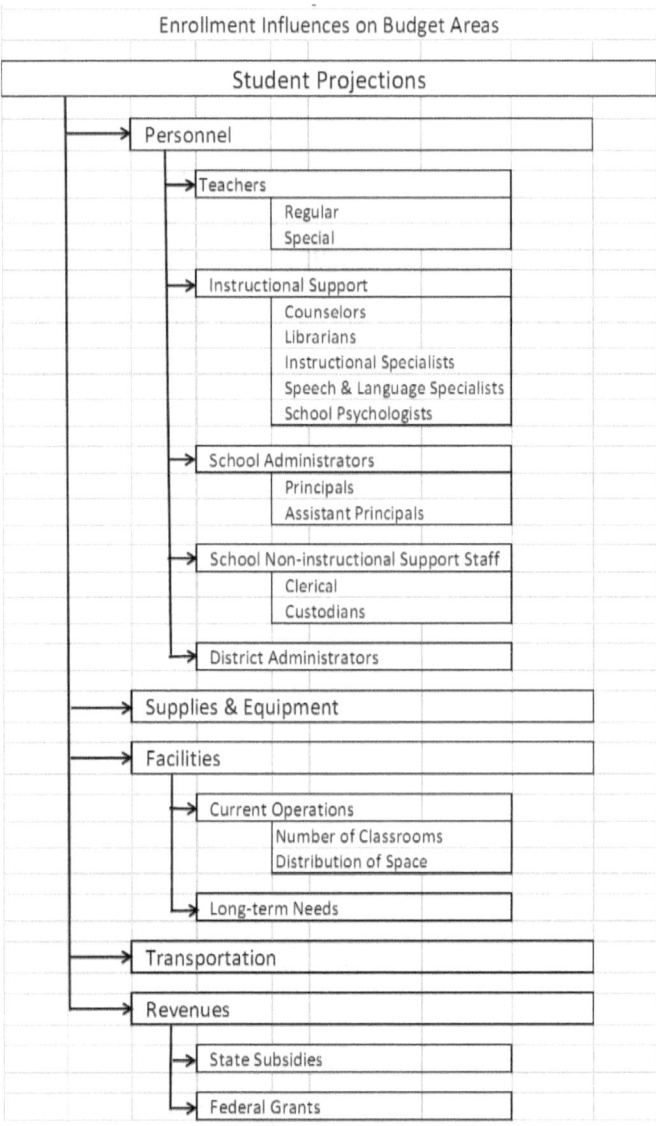

Figure 2.1. Linkages between Student Enrollments and Budgets

Most types of personnel requirements are derived directly or indirectly from estimates of the *number of students* to be served. Establishing the suitable number of various types of personnel is generally driven by student enrollment projections at different grade levels and for different student classes, courses, and needs. For teachers and instructional support personnel, districts often have board-established policies for acceptable student-to-staff ratios.

For example, the number of teachers required is frequently determined using the estimated enrollments and district student/teacher policies. Similar determinations are made for other professional instructional and management personnel and district policies concerning expected caseloads.

- Nonpersonnel Items. Allocations to schools for instructional books and supplies, materials, and equipment are frequently made on a dollar-per-student basis. Coupled with the projected student enrollments, this provides a pool of money to the school that can be used by the principal and teachers to provide these instructional resources.
- Transportation. The numbers of buses and driver/maintenance staff required are affected by student enrollments and bussing routes, schedules, and distances. Minimizing the number of buses—subject to students' safety, quality of service, and district policies—has important budgetary implications.

For example, the distribution of students among elementary, middle, and high schools—and the location of those schools—affect bus transportation routes; location of students, combined with district policies on walk-to-school distances, will determine those students eligible for transportation services; ride time limitations, particularly in sparsely populated areas, may lead to more inefficient and costly operations.

The number of students attending schools outside their attendance zone to attend specialized placements also affects transportation needs. In some states, public schools must also transport resident students attending private or charter schools outside district boundaries.

- Revenues. On the revenue side, budget estimates of certain revenue sources may also be directly related to the number of students, *with varying needs*, in the school district and each school. Specific state subsidies and/or federal aid, which are distributed to districts on a dollar-per-student basis, are determined by multiplying the number of students by the dollar-per-student aid amount. In some cases, these subsidies may be based on the yearly number of certain categories of students, such as poverty status or disability. This effort will require district enrollment estimates of these subgroups of students for budgeting projected revenues.
- Facilities. The needs for facilities, such as number of schools and/or classrooms and laboratories (not to mention computer centers and libraries and other rooms, both currently and long term), are calculated using the projected student enrollments. Estimates of schools and other district

instructional and administrative facilities are long-term decisions. Table 2.1 provides an illustration of this procedure along with several enrollment-to-budget instances from other areas that are driven by projected enrollments.

As an illustration, if an elementary school were projected to have 500 students for the upcoming year, district administrators could then apply the district's student-to-staff ratios to estimate the amount/numbers of staff and facilities requirements needed for the upcoming year (and related costs). In the example, with a maximum capacity of twenty-five students per classroom, the school of 500 students would need a minimum of about twenty-five classroom teachers to serve its students' classrooms.

Practically, this ratio would mean implementing the policy, using an average classroom size for the school with some classrooms having slightly more or fewer students than the policy specifies due to actual numbers of students per grade.

Instructional specialists often have assigned caseloads of students and can serve students in multiple schools. Given the district's staffing policy for math specialists of a caseload of 200 students, the district would assign 2.5 math specialists to the school. Likely the 0.5 specialist in Edison Elementary would also be assigned to another school for the other 0.5 FTE for the position.

Table 2.1. Examples of Enrollments to Budget Items

Edison Elementary School Projected Students		Current 500 students	in Five Years 400 students
Budget Item	Student to Staff Ratio	Staff Required	Staff Required
Classroom Teacher	20	25	20
Math Specialist	200	2.5	2
Speech & Language Specialist	250	2	1.6
Classrooms	20	25	20
	$/Student		
Instructional Supplies	$75	$37,500	$30,000
Equipment	$50	$25,000	$20,000
State General Education Subsidy	$5,000	$2,500,000	$2,000,000

(Note: The $/student amount would be applied to all students in the district, not just those in this school to estimate district revenues from the state.)

If all teachers had their own classroom, the school would have to have twenty-five classrooms to house its students. The students will also generate funds for instructional supplies and equipment for use by teachers in their classrooms. District policies often establish an amount per student to be provided to schools through their budget. In this example, with an allocation of $75 per student for supplies, the school would receive $37,500 more to provide these instructional items for 500 students in the school.

Transportation is a budget item that is also tied to the number of students to be served, along with (a) where they live and distance from home to school and back; (b) what schools they attend; and (c) a variety of district policies regarding their needs for transportation. All of these variables combine into a bus schedule and routing plan to determine the number of buses that will be needed to provide the necessary services to the kids.

At an annual operating cost of $50,000 to $100,000 per bus, these services—whether provided by the district or contracted to a bus company vendor—are expensive and are derived from student enrollment projections and geographic district layout.

CONTEXT FOR MAKING STUDENT ENROLLMENT PROJECTIONS

- Counting Students. Several different approaches can be used in counting the number of students by age and needs in a school district. The approach selected will probably be determined by state department of education's student accounting definitions. The two main approaches to measuring the number of students are average daily membership (ADM) and average daily attendance (ADA).

ADM counts all students enrolled in school (i.e., on the *membership* list)—whether or not they are actually attending school at the time the student count is taken. ADA, by contrast, counts only those students actually attending school at the time that the count is made. Thus, ADM is *average daily membership* as those registered in the school building.

The difference between the two approaches is how they treat students' absences; ADM (membership) counts include the absent students when the enrollment is determined, while the ADA (attendance) counts exclude absences, counting only those students physically present at the time the enrollment is determined. As a result, ADM counts will always be higher than ADA counts, a situation that disadvantages school districts with high absentee rates.

With the higher count, budgets based on ADM plan for the full complement of students served by the school or district and provide a cushion in terms of instructional staff and resources and classroom space for days where a higher number of students may be in attendance. Modifications to the basic approaches are possible, including *excused* absences as part of ADA counts, for example.

Another differentiation that may be made in student counts is enrollments versus full-time equivalent (FTE) counts. Enrollment generally corresponds to head counts of students, where every student enrolled in a program counts as one student, whether full time or part time. FTE counts adjust the number of students reported only to include the actual amount of time in a program. The students who participate part time in a particular program are counted only for that *fraction of time* in that program.

For example, in a student accounting system utilizing FTE counts, a student with a mild disability—receiving special education in a resource room for one period out of five periods in the school day—would have an FTE count of 0.20 in special education and 0.80 in regular education. This allocates the student count for students by the time they spend in different programs and grade levels.

ADM counts provide a more appropriate estimate of students for districts to plan and budget for programs; ADA or FTE student counts do not necessarily correspond to the resources, and space districts must provide for all students, whether they are in attendance on a particular day. The special education student in the previous example will probably require a full complement of services in regular education, even though the FTE enrollment is only 0.80.

The period each day spent outside the classroom (e.g., in a resource room setting) is of very little budgetary significance to the regular classroom: the teacher is paid the same, the student's desk remains and takes up the same space, and heat and light consumption are not reduced. Perhaps some instructional materials are not required, but these are usually quite minor. As a result, school districts operating under an ADA or FTE approach may have to maintain two separate, but related, student accounting procedures—one for state reporting and one for local planning and budgeting.

- Who Does the Projections—and When? Enrollment projections are usually done centrally for the school district, either by district office personnel or through a contract arrangement with an outside consultant. School principals or district department heads can contribute information to the projection process if they have useful knowledge or insights about unusual circumstances that affect the number of students leaving or entering the school in the upcoming year. Projections are generally done early in the

school year so that they can be utilized in the district's budget process. Often the process will begin in August or September with data gathering by the business office.
- What Information Is Needed? The central office personnel responsible for developing projections will collect internal information maintained by the district, such as the up-to-date enrollment numbers in the district and in each school, demographic characteristics of current students, numbers and location of special needs students. Additional external information from the community that will influence the number of students should be gathered during this time as well.

Possible items would include new or expanding housing developments; planned or announced major private-sector company changes such as new business opening or expanding in the district; or manufacturing plants or other businesses closing or relocating outside of the district. The impacts of economic activity in the community on future enrollments, both positive and negative, should also be incorporated into the enrollment projection process.

Another important issue for student enrollment projections is the general student population trends in the district and state. A historical review of five or more past years of enrollment trends can provide important insight into potential future changes. Some questions to ask are the following: (a) Has the number of students been growing (or steady or declining) in the district in recent years? (b) Are the enrollment trends the same for the elementary level as for the high school level? and (c) What have been the birth rates in the district's catchment area? In many ways, districts have a relatively long lead time to adjust for enrollment changes. Students who will be entering kindergarten next year have already been born five years ago, ample time to plan for staffing and facilities changes.

The upper-level elementary students will progress into junior and senior high school year after year; again, the numbers and timing of their entry are known well ahead of time. However, we will have no changes, as students advance through the system, or that there will be no migration into and/or out of the district. However, a relatively reliable baseline estimate of future student enrollments can be determined from past trends and analyzing potential changes that would alter the past patterns.

- Types of Students for Projections. To build the budget for the next fiscal year, detailed estimates of the number of students to be served in the school district for the upcoming year are needed. These projections generally are made along several dimensions relevant to educational and budgetary decisions—for example, district total, education level (elementary, middle, high school), school building, grade level, and type of student (e.g., regular, exceptional, English Language Learner/Limited English Proficiency, vocational, disabled, and disadvantaged).

These divisions are not mutually exclusive and may overlap within the district—or at a given school—to provide greater detail about the students expected for the upcoming year and any particular resource needs that may be required.

Consequently, the categories used by the school district to project next year's student enrollments should correspond to the instructional and instructional support programs that the district is planning to provide its students. For example, to meet the curriculum, staffing, and instructional space needs, it may be necessary to estimate enrollments of disabled students in multiple dimensions—by exceptionality, by type of instructional and support program, by location, and by service provider (district, contracted special education service organization). This is not to say that every possible permutation of enrollment should be calculated, but that some may be useful subprojections that focus on student populations of particular interest and needs.

- Distribution and Use of Projections. Once the student and staffing projections are completed, the relevant results are provided to the district personnel who are developing the budget requests for each program or organizational area. For example, estimates of individual school enrollments, in total, by grade level and by relevant demographic groups are frequently given to building principals to use in their budget preparation activities.

Likewise, the special education director would receive estimates of the number of students with disabling conditions (by type of disability, age, and severity of condition) to establish a baseline for developing a budget request in that area. The enrollment projections would then be used to estimate total personnel requirements and allocation of positions among different grades or types of students, as well as to determine the amount of money available for instructional supplies and equipment.

ENROLLMENT PROJECTION TECHNIQUES

Several different methods are often used for estimating student enrollments for the upcoming year—and beyond. The approaches range from simple to sophisticated and vary in their reliability.

1. Educated Guess: The simplest approach is an "educated guess" by the district superintendent, business manager, school principals, and/or others, based on the current enrollments and their projections about what may occur next year.

This approach is fast, inexpensive, and understandable—and useful. It can also incorporate relevant information about district economic, social, or political conditions into the enrollment estimates. On the other hand, it is also subject to considerable error or bias, since the estimates are often derived from past experience and subjective assessments.

Other more formalized projection approaches have been successful in estimating student enrollments, including various mathematical forecasting techniques used for projecting future enrollments based on past trends.[1] However, the basic rationale underlying these extrapolative techniques is the assumption that the same conditions affecting enrollment in the past will continue to prevail in the future. This approach may not be the case in districts undergoing demographic, social, and economic changes.

For example, a district that has been economically depressed and losing population for the past several years may *not* want to project a decreasing enrollment trend into the next years if, for example, several manufacturing firms have opened up new plants in the community requiring new employees—and the economy and demography are showing signs of recovering.

2. Examine the Background: The assumptions and conditions behind enrollment projections should be examined to see if they are still valid in the light of what administrators know or believe about the district's condition in the upcoming years. Adjustments can and should be made to the projections calculated by any of the forecasting techniques to reflect more accurately the expected changes in the district's future.
3. Trend-Line Analysis. Trend-line analysis is a form of linear regression that uses the year as the predictor variable and the district enrollment as the dependent outcome or predicted variable. With a spreadsheet or a simple statistical program on a computer, it is possible to calculate future enrollments easily. The data needed are the enrollments of the pertinent student populations for each of the past five or six years.

Future years' levels are estimated by projecting the trend line from the past years' data—and extending it into future years. The statistical methodology of linear regression is used to calculate the line of "best fit" for the previous enrollments. The result is an equation of a straight line. This is represented by the trend line in Table 2.2:

Table 2.2. Trend Line Analysis Projection Example

Historical Enrollments		Projected Enrollments	
Year	Students	Year	Students
2012	13,142	2017	13,288
2013	13,029	2018	13,326
2014	13,195	2019	13,365
2015	13,309		
2016	13,193		

CONCLUSION

Thus, estimating starts the financial progress—leading from an informed, intelligent guess to a reality—as critical steps in district and school finance. This chapter has made concrete suggestions and used some real numbers to start the budgeting and finance process. Money needs raising, allocating, and tracing from the sources to the kids in the school classroom with their teachers and other staff—and equipment.

Bruce S. Cooper led the way back in 1993 in tracking bucks to the classroom and the kids, as explained: "Once funding data are classified and determined by function, the model was found to be 'user friendly', district found it easy and useful to track the dollars to the classroom and pupils" (p. 2, *School site funding and tracking*, 1994).

NOTE

1. For a discussion of enrollment projection techniques, see Faith E. Crampton, R. Craig Wood, & David C. Thompson, *Money and schools*, 6th edition (New York: Routledge, 2015).

REFERENCE

Cooper, B. S. (1994). Micro-Financial Model in 23 Districts in Ten States. 2nd Revision. Paper originally presented at the Annual Meeting of the American Education Finance Association (Albuquerque, NM, March 18, 1993).

Chapter 3

Personnel

Education Is a People Enterprise

INTRODUCTION

Education finance is primarily about the varied costs of *personnel*: for example, people who teach, counsel and advise, lead, and perform other tasks in and about the school buildings and school system. As *About Education* explains,

> It truly does take an army to raise and educate a child. The most recognizable employees within a school district are the teachers. However, they represent only a portion of the personnel that works within the school. School personnel can be divided into three distinct categories including school leaders, faculty, and support staff. (1995, p. 1)

Thus, school leaders need to understand the costs and pay levels for teachers (mainly), other administrators, and a range of support and maintenance staff in their schools. This chapter examines the costs, percentages, and skills necessary to manage, plan, and evaluate staff and their costs in schools. For education is a people enterprise, and as such, funding for teachers, administrators, and other personnel is central.

UNDERSTANDING THE FIELD OF SCHOOL FINANCE AND LEADERSHIP

Let's start with a set of key definitions related to personnel and funding of staff and leaders in school systems. Here are some key concepts.

Definitions

A "Certified school instructor" means a teacher or instructional support provider. These teachers and support staff are critical to the instruction and learning of the students.

B "Certified school employee" or "certified school personnel" means a licensed school employee.

C "Licensed school employee" means teachers, school administrators, and instructional support providers.

D "Instructional support provider" means a person who is employed to support the instructional program of a school district, including educational assistant, librarian, school counselor, social worker, school nurse, speech-language pathologist, psychologist, physical therapist, occupational therapist, recreational therapist, interpreter for the deaf and diagnostician.

E "Teacher" means a person who holds a level one, two, or three-A teaching license and whose primary duty is classroom instruction or the supervision, below the school principal level, of an instructional program.

F "School employee" is licensed and nonlicensed employees of the district.

G "School principal" means the chief instructional leader and administrative head of a public or private school.

H "School administrator" means a person licensed to administer in the district and includes school principal and central office administrators.

I "Substitute teacher" means a person who holds a state-issued certificate to substitute for a teacher in the classroom. According to an article in *EdNext*, teachers miss a small but regular number of days, about ten days, or 5 percent of the regular 180 days, requiring substitute teacher to be used.

In particular, as Kronholz (2017) explains,

> According to a 2009–2010 report from the U.S. Department of Education based on data from surveys of 57,000 schools, U.S. teachers take off an average of 9.4 days each or 5% of regular school days, during a typical 180-day school year, and substitute teachers are called to fill in for absent teachers. This means that the average public school student has substitute teachers for more than six months of his or her school career. In a new analysis, June Kronholz discusses recent research on teacher absences and the impact that the reliance on substitutes has on school budgets and student learning. (p. 3)

"Discharge" means the act of severing the employment relationship with a certified school employee prior to the expiration of the current employment contract.

K "Terminate" means, in the case of a certified school employee, the act of not reemploying an employee for the ensuring school year and, in the case of a noncertified school employee, the act of severing the employment relationship with the employee.

As J. Chambers and William J. Fowler explain,

> Most educators readily acknowledge that schools districts in different geographic locations encounter *different costs* in acquiring and retaining similarly qualified [and high quality] teachers. Teacher salaries reflect not only the cost-of-living in a geographic labor market, but also a school district's preference for teachers who are better educated or more experienced. (2017, p. 2)

And here's a summary of the cost and effects of substitute teachers:

- Duke University researchers Charles Clotfelter, Helen Ladd, and Jacob Vigdor found that being taught by a sub for ten days per year has a larger effect on a child's math scores than if the child changed schools, and about half the size of the difference between students from well-to-do and poor families.
- Columbia University researchers Mariesa Herrmann and Jonah Rockoff (2011) concluded that the effect on learning of using a substitute for even a day is greater than the effect of replacing an average teacher with a terrible one—that is, a teacher in the tenth percentile for math instruction and the twentieth percentile in English instruction.

These and other recent studies find the following:

- Teachers in bigger schools were absent more often than those in smaller schools.
- Teachers in low-income schools were absent more often than those serving higher-income families.
- Elementary school teachers took off more time than did those in high schools.
- Tenured teachers took off 3.7 more days than did those without tenure.
- Female teachers under age thirty-five averaged 3.2 more absences than did men.
- Teachers who had a master's degree or graduated from a competitive college took less leave then those who didn't.
- Teachers in traditional districts take off more time than those in charters. Thirty-seven percent of teachers are absent more than ten days at district elementary and middle schools compared to 22 percent at charters.

Many school systems are plagued with dysfunctional human resources management systems. To understand how this dysfunction affects the quality of education and school finance, we must understand the impact on schools, students, teachers, and administrators. Examples of the dysfunctions include the following:

- Pay checks arrive late
- Pay checks contain wrong amounts
- People who are not on payroll getting paid
- Performance evaluations may not reflect true performance
- Poor or inaccurate or inadequate record keeping

Subsequently, we must ask, "How do these problems affect the following?"

- Recruitment
- Hiring
- Development
- Compensation especially in terms of "Pay for Performance"
- Retaining Talent

CONCLUSION

Finally, we must recommend possible solutions. These solutions may include the following: First, cast a wide net and do not allow top talent to get away. We can seek talent from these major sources:

- National organizations with reputation for recruiting and training top talented educators and administrators such as:
- New Teacher Project
  - Teach for America
  - New School Leaders for New Schools
  - Broad Foundation Urban School Leaders Program
  - Academy for Urban School Leadership
  - Peace Corps
  - Military organization.
- Universities that educate and train top teachers, principals, and administrators include such as these New York and New Jersey universities:
  - Montclair State University
  - Columbia University
  - Syracuse University
  - CUNY—City University of New York provides tuition reimbursement for teachers who become certified in math and science.

The second possible solution is having the human resources department use online services to become a true "customer-service center." Use online systems to automate the application and selection process. Link these processes to payroll systems to save time, money, and improve customer service to help to retain, attract, and hire talent.

The third possible solution is to focus on rigorous training and retention because nationwide about 30 percent of new teachers leave the profession within the first five years. We can address this problem by providing sound *mentoring* especially for new hires (see Cooper & McCray, 2016; McCray & Cooper, 2016). We must link benchmarks to state teaching standards.

Fourth, we must maintain sound leadership especially at the top. We must maintain sustainable and continuous district leadership. Schools must hire and retain top superintendent and business administrators. Moreover, district leaders must forge and maintain strong links to the local community and government.

Fifth, schools must get unions and district leadership to work together and achieve long-term collaboration. Some of the ways to accomplish this collaboration is to work together to lobby state and federal governments to fully fund all mandates.

If a district wants to attract, hire, develop, and retain the best teacher talent possible, then the human resources department must be state of the art. The human resources departments must use up-to-date technology because hiring the top talent in the twenty-first century requires the use of twenty-first-century technology and tools. Schools might consider teacher performance pay that is in practice or under discussion in many states. However, the most common approach is test-based pay for performance.

We must examine the underlying assumptions such as somehow teachers will try harder if they are motivated by the chance to earn additional money. But this assumes teachers are not trying hard now! It also assumes that teachers somehow know what to do but simply are not or will not perform at a higher level without the prospect of more money.

However, this assumes that teachers are motivated more by money than meeting their students' educational needs. This begs the following questions: (1) How do we define performance pay? (2) How do we know that students actually are learning more simply by scoring higher or well on statewide tests? and (3) What other criteria can be used besides money to incentivize teachers and teaching? A pay-for-performance compensation system requires definition before it is implemented! Schools must understand what students and teachers think about this.

Hence, a district should determine what it seeks to accomplish with its *performance pay system* and how all affected employees will contribute to and meet the goals. Most importantly, if performance pay is based on student performance, then student performance must also be defined. Measures of student performance must be developed that answer these questions:

- Do scores on standardized tests indicate any of the student's skill level, knowledge, or ability to succeed in life and contribute to society?
- If these points are true, then how do we create students who:
  - are life long learners;
  - have the skills to succeed in life;
  - are critical thinkers;
  - have "twenty-first-century" skills;
  - are problem solvers and;
  - reach their full potential?

Then students can pursue different paths in life based on their individual interests and abilities.

GOING FORWARD: THE NECESSITY OF KEEPING GOOD LEADERS

In conclusion, besides the quality and value to schools of good teachers, we should also be aware of the need for good leaders to remain in their jobs within their schools and the costs of replacing a school principal, the key leader at the building level (see Scott, 2014). A study found that leader-turnover was a critical problem in schools: "Some of those principals left on their own. Some were removed." According to a new report from the nonprofit School Leaders Network, half of new principals quit in their third year on the job.

And as one administrator reported,

> Heather Wolpert-Gawron has been teaching for eleven years at Jefferson Middle School in San Gabriel, Calif. During that time, she says, the school has had about ten principals. The group, which provides training and support to principals, says the job has become too complex and isolating. Principals put in long hours overseeing teachers, meeting with parents and implementing one reform after another.

REFERENCES

Analysis/Methodology Report (October 1995). *Public school teacher cost differences across the United States.* Washington, DC: About Education, 2017.

Chambers, J., Jr. & Fowler, W. J. (2017). *A comprehensive breakdown of the roles of school personnel.* Washington, DC: American Institutes for Research, National Center for Education Statistics.

Cooper, B. S., & McCray, C. (2016). *Mentoring for better education*. Lanham, MD: Rowman & Littlefield.
Kronholz, J. (2013). Substitute teachers are a large presence in American schools. http://educationnext.org/substitute-teachers-are-a-large-presence-inamerican-schools/.
Herrmann, M. A., & Rockoff, J. E. (2011). Worker absence and productivity: Evidence from teaching, *Journal of Labor Economics*, *122* (561), 749–782.
McCray, C. & Cooper, B. S. (2016). *Mentoring with meaning: How educators can be more professional and effective*. Lanham, MD: Rowman & Littlefield.
Scott, A. (2014). *The high cost of principal turnover*. SmartBriefs. Washington, DC: ASCD.

Chapter 4

Special Education

Special Program Needs Budgeting

INTRODUCTION

Individuals with Disabilities Education Act (IDEA) is the chief legislative and mandated program and service driver for special needs students in education. However, IDEA has been underfunded since its passage in 1975. Although President Obama promised full funding of IDEA, he did not seek or get full funding. The president's FY-2017 budget funds IDEA at FY-2016 levels of only 16 percent of the full cost of all IDEA special education mandated programs and services.

This chapter focuses on the needs of special education, its costs at the federal and local levels, and steps to improve the program for special education students, and the higher costs. For the underfunding IDEA at only 16 percent is less than half of the federal government's original 40 percent limit on funding students with educational and physiological disabilities.

Moreover, the federal government promised to pay only 40 percent of the national average per-special education pupil expenditure penalizing districts with higher than average per-pupil special education expenditures. The highest funding level provided by the federal government for funding IDEA's mandated programs and services was 18 percent in 2005. This means that President Obama's proposed funding level for FY-2017 is below that of more than a decade ago under President Bush.

National funding IDEA at only 16 percent means 84 percent must be paid for by local and state public school districts nationwide because IDEA's programs and services are mandated. Mandated programs and services require any funding deficit to be funded by the local public school districts. Therefore, underfunding IDEA requires districts to make up for the funding shortfall by cutting nonmandate-protected programs and services. Underfunding IDEA is one of the most powerful drivers of public school district budget cuts nationwide.

Moreover, the chronic underfunding of IDEA and the budget cuts it fosters often pit regular and special education parents, students, and teachers against one another in a battle for scarce financial, material, and human educational resources.

Key Question: *Why shouldn't the federal government be required to pay 100 percent of its national special education policy mandates?*
The answer: Special education expenses are one of the fastest growing financial challenges confronting school districts nationwide—and particularly in New Jersey. School districts throughout New Jersey pay not only all of the general expense for their special education students but also the majority of the "excess cost" of special education.

"Excess cost" is defined as the per-pupil expenses of special education that exceed the regular per-student cost. Declining state and federal aid not only has increased the proportion of property taxes used to fund schools but also has heightened the pressure to find necessary resources perhaps by reducing programs and services for regular education students in order to fund mandate-protected programs and services such as special education.

Special education costs are driven primarily by expensive out-of-district placements, mandated preschool programs (including intensive services for autistic students), and lower special education student to staff ratios as well as by parents suing school districts to obtain private school placements for their children.

The legal fees for such lawsuits account for another escalating expense for schools. In addition, if a school district loses in a New Jersey administrative court, the district has to pay not only the judgment costs but also all of the plaintiff's legal costs regardless of the length of the trial. It seems as if holding New Jersey school districts harmless from such lawsuits would be another way in which to enable school districts to allocate more of their scarce resources to instruction.

Many districts find that out-of-district placements can consume as much as 50 percent of the special education budget. The students placed in out-of-district schools tend to be the most expensive because they are usually the children most in need of special education programs and services. Depending on the student's disability, the annual cost of sending a student to an out-of-district private school can range from roughly $60,000 to over $250,000, especially for the most educationally and physically challenged students.

The federal government forces its traditional public schools to pay for an ever-increasing proportion of special education costs by underfunding IDEA mandates. IDEA's underfunding forces districts to increase local property taxes and identify funds to offset the shortfall through means that adversely impact the regular education budget. Underfunded IDEA mandates can result in much larger class sizes as school districts are forced to consider reducing regular education teachers and aides. Larger class sizes often lead to lower test scores, which make it more difficult for students, schools, and districts to achieve academic progress.

And each new administration may have a different view of the federal role: President Trump is a good current example, as one source reports:

> That blueprint includes reducing so-called formula funding in education by 10 percent, or $2.3 billion, for federal programs like Title I whose aid is allotted mainly according to fixed formulas; cutting competitive and project grant funding under the Every Student Succeeds Act by $1.8 billion; and phasing out Head Start by cutting 10 percent from the program each year, or $935 million in the first year. (Head Start, which serves preschoolers from poor families, is overseen by the Department of Health and Human Services, not the Education Department.)
>
> In the current year's budget, Title I for disadvantaged students is the largest single piece of federal K-12 spending, at $14.9 billion, followed by Individuals with Disabilities Education Act state grants, at $11.9 billion. (Andrew Ujifusa, 2017, p. 3)

Although the Heritage budget calls for a 10 percent cut to formula-funded education programs, the director of the think tank's Center for Education Policy, Lindsey Burke, said it wants to look at allocating IDEA money differently but isn't calling for cuts in that aid at this time.

Unless public school districts nationwide not only wish to avoid IDEA-driven continued budget cuts to offset IDEA's underfunding and a downward spiral in the quality of education stemming from IDEA's underfunding but also higher local property taxes, then the districts nationwide should ban together and demand the federal government fund IDEA 100 percent, and, therefore, pay for all of the costs of IDEA's mandated programs and services.

Moreover, fully funding IDEA would prevent the budget cuts it currently fosters. Stopping IDEA-driven budget cuts would end the conflict among regular and special education parents, students, and teachers over scarce financial, material, and human educational resources, and put the focus on working together to provide a quality education for all.

CONCLUSION

Thus, recommendation number one is clearly: *Have the fed's pay for special education costs.*

Recommendation two: *Do it now:* IDEA reauthorization is seven years past due! Even with the 84 percent underfunding of IDEA, the federal government's special education program mandates that LEAs, local school districts, fund the unfunded portion or 84 percent. Many scholars, particularly Dr. Bruce Baker (2011), have found that the federal underfunding of IDEA drives budget gaps and causes other nonmandate-protected programs and services to be cut, especially in large urban districts!

Recommendations are thus: IDEA needs *reauthorization* and *full funding*; both will help districts avoid severe budget cuts and staff reductions!

Let's focus our special ed chapter on IDEA, and how its 84 percent underfunding drives other budgetary shortfalls in districts! We need all hands on deck, if we are to assistant teachers and administrators in special education, now and in the future.

REFERENCES

Baker, B. D. (2011, February 4). Where's the pork? Mitigating the damage of state aid cuts [Weblog post]. Retrieved from http://www.schoolfinance101.wordpress.com.

Ujifusa, A. (2017, February 7). Big stakes for K-12 as federal budget process gears up. *Education Week*, pp. 1–3.

Chapter 5

State Education Aid

How to Budget and Manage State Funding

INTRODUCTION

Because education is primarily a state responsibility—according to the U.S. Constitution and the fifty states' constitutions—the nation has fifty different educational systems. Laws, curricula, standards, school organization, and testing are in part set by the state legislatures, governors, courts, and state education agencies and carried out in the nation's approximately 14,000 local school systems. As the U.S. Census reported in 2012,

> School districts are public school systems that provide regular, special, and/ or vocational education services for children in pre-kindergarten through 12th grade. Public school systems in the United States are locally administered, and their geographic structure varies by state and region.
>
> Most districts in the Mid-Atlantic and New England states follow county, township, or city boundaries, while districts in the Midwest and Western states are generally independent of municipal boundaries and frequently intersect statistical areas like Census tracts and block groups. The U.S. has more than 14,000 public school districts and spends more than $500 billion on public elementary and secondary education each year (combined spending of federal, state, and local governments).

While the states are all under the U.S. Constitution—for example, national laws and regulations, and receive 11 percent from federal funding—the structure and operation of schools have mostly been left to the states, which now pay the second *largest percentage of total education funding—with local and federal funding coming in most cases at a lower percent and level.* Each state must "raise the money" through taxation, and then divvy it up among the local school districts (except Hawaii that is a one statewide-district), and set goals, performance levels, testing, and outcomes.

This chapter explores the key role of the states in funding U.S. public schools. And with fifty states and the District of Columbia (DC), local district leaders need a close contact and understanding of *their own state's* level of school district funding, equity, and regulation and standards.

Thus, states are quite different, in some ways, concerning how they raise and use funds for K–12 education. This chapter examines various attempts to equalize school funding across and within the fifty states and the District of Columbia. Two states are perhaps the most different. For example, Hawaii has local district funding at a high level with $5.9 billion state spending and $3.8 billion local, while Hawaii has no direct local funding or governance of schools at all, with one state school system, one school board, and school superintendent (statewide), and thus one education budget in Honolulu for the whole state.

Hawaii has little local funding (only $3 billion raised locally); no local elections; and no local school boards, with the state contributing $11 billion toward schools. Odd, because Hawaii is also the most physically and geographically broken-up, divided state in the United States, with five different islands, separated by the Pacific Ocean. As Roth (2015) reports:

> The *Hawaii State Department of Education* is the only statewide public education system in the United States. The school district can be thought of as analogous to the school districts of other cities and communities in the United States, but in some manners can also be thought of as analogous to the state education agencies of other states. As the official state education agency, the Hawaii State Department of Education oversees all 283 public schools and charter schools and over 13,000 teachers in the State of Hawaii. (pp. 1–8)

To understand the differences among the fifty states in the governance and funding of schools, we raise these issues and questions: "To do this, we first classify governance relative to three main components:

- The degree to which decision-making authority lies at the state versus the local level.
- The degree to which decision-making authority is distributed among many institutions versus consolidated in a few.
- The degree to which the public can participate in the policymaking process." (Zeehandelaar & Griffith, et al., 2015, p. 3)

We score states on each component and then combine them into eight "governance types," named for the characteristics they have in common with some of history's most famous political leaders and theorists.

So while all states are bound by federal laws, policies, and programs, each state sets its own organizational, financial models, levels and types of taxation, and, thus, has different amounts, rankings, and per-pupil levels of resources and spending. Table 5.1 shows the fifty states in terms of per-pupil spending, based on financial income and number of students.

FUNDING

As we saw in the previous chapter, approximately 44 percent of a school district's revenue comes from local funds, primarily from house and business property taxes. States are a major source of revenue for schools, contributing the overall level of school resources. States have the authority to levy a variety of taxes in the form of personal and corporate income taxes, general sales taxes, motor fuel taxes, utility taxes, and alcohol and tobacco taxes, to name the major ones. In most cases, this tax money is placed in a general revenue fund to be distributed to a multitude of competing governmental bodies, including public schools.

How much revenue public schools receive from the state depends upon the state. Some states have constitutionally mandated amounts that go to public education. For example, a state constitution may mandate that 25 percent of the state's general revenue must be allocated to education. According to the National Center for Education Statistics report in school year 2010–2011, in twenty states, at least half of education revenues came from state governments, a rather significant amount. Nationally, schools received an average of 44 percent in school year 2010–2011 from state sources, a decrease from the 50 percent in school year 2000–2001.

Thus, we are truly the United States of America in educational provision, with each state being its own education system and funding. When comparing state revenues for education with local revenues (see Table 6.1), we note the degree to which most school systems depend on state aid, in addition to the local spending levels. Overall, in 2015, the United States spent $1,648.3 billion from state sources, total, and $1,159.7 billion from local sources (mostly from local property taxes). Total at the state and local levels of spending on public education, K–12, was $2.8 trillion in the United States in 2015.

Only three states—Tennessee, Louisiana, and Nebraska—are different, as their spending percentages and levels are higher locally than at the state level; or perhaps the statement should be: local spending in these three states in 2015 was and is higher than the state contributions.

Table 5.1. Spending by Fifty States on Education (in Trillions of Dollars in 2015): TOTAL: STATE AND LOCAL: $ 2.8 TRILLION.

All States Combined, 2015	$1,648.3 Billion	$1,159.7 Billion
State	State Revenue	Local Revenue (Billions $)
Alabama	$21.0	$15.0
Alaska	$6.9	$2.7
Arizona	$24.8	$20.5
Arkansas	$15.7	$3.9
California	$262.7	$184.2
Colorado	$24.7	$22.4
Connecticut	$28.3	$14.4
Delaware	$7.7	$2.1
District of Columbia	$-0.2	$10.0
Florida	$74.4	$67.6
Georgia	$37.4	$29.2
Hawaii	$11.0	$3.0
Idaho	$7.1	$3.3
Illinois	$64.5	$46.2
Indiana	$26.2	$16.6
Iowa	$15.9	$10.6
Kansas	$13.7	$9.5
Kentucky	$20.0	$9.7
Louisiana	$21.0	$29.0
Maine	$6.4	$2.6
Maryland	$32.0	$21.7
Massachusetts	$41.8	$-2.6
Michigan	$49.4	$25.4
Minnesota	$40.1	$20.1
Mississippi	$13.2	$8.4
Missouri	$23.4	$18.6
Montana	$5.9	$2.4
Nebraska	$7.9	$11.0
Nevada	$12.2	$8.1
New Hampshire	$5.9	$3.8
New Jersey	$50.1	$36.9
New Mexico	$11.2	$3.9
New York	$137.3	$124.7
North Carolina	$45.7	$32.6
North Dakota	$9.4	$2.3
Ohio	$58.4	$34.9
Oklahoma	$18.0	$10.0
Oregon	$22.9	$12.7
Pennsylvania	$62.4	$37.3
Rhode Island	$6.1	$4.0

All States Combined, 2015	$1,648.3 Billion	$1,159.7 Billion
	State	State Revenue	Local Revenue (Billions $)
	Tennessee	$22.8	$24.8
	Texas	$109.5	$93.8
	Utah	$12.6	$8.1
	Vermont	$4.9	$1.2
	Virginia	$37.8	$25.5
	Washington	$37.4	$27.8
	West Virginia	$9.6	$3.5
	Wisconsin	$30.6	$18.7
	Wyoming	$4.6	$3.4
(All states combined)	$1,648.3	$1,159.7	

As Kenyon (2007) explained:

Property taxation and school funding are closely linked in the United States, with nearly half of all property tax revenue used for public elementary and secondary education. There is an active policy debate across the country regarding the degree to which public schools should be funded with property tax dollars.

Some policy makers and analysts call for reduced reliance on property tax revenue and increased reliance on state funding; others claim that the property tax is a critical ingredient in effective local government. School funding is no less controversial, and nearly every state has dealt with school funding litigation and court mandates at least once over the last several decades. (p. 1)

The major plans for distributing state revenue include some type of foundation formula, guaranteed tax base, equalizing formula, or combination thereof. Since no two state plans for distributing revenue are the same, it is not feasible to discuss all the plans. Plus, with the current trend of litigation regarding adequate and equitable funding, plans are often subject to change.

FEDERAL SOURCES

Meanwhile, the U.S. (federal) spending on K–12 education has stayed fairly stable over the past fifty or so years, as shown in figure 5.1.

In this chapter we will examine the concept of distributing money based on adequacy and equity. Many plans incorporate local wealth factors and some form of student attendance, whether it is average daily attendance (ADA) or average daily membership (ADM). School leaders understand that students' daily attendance is important for the student educationally. Understanding

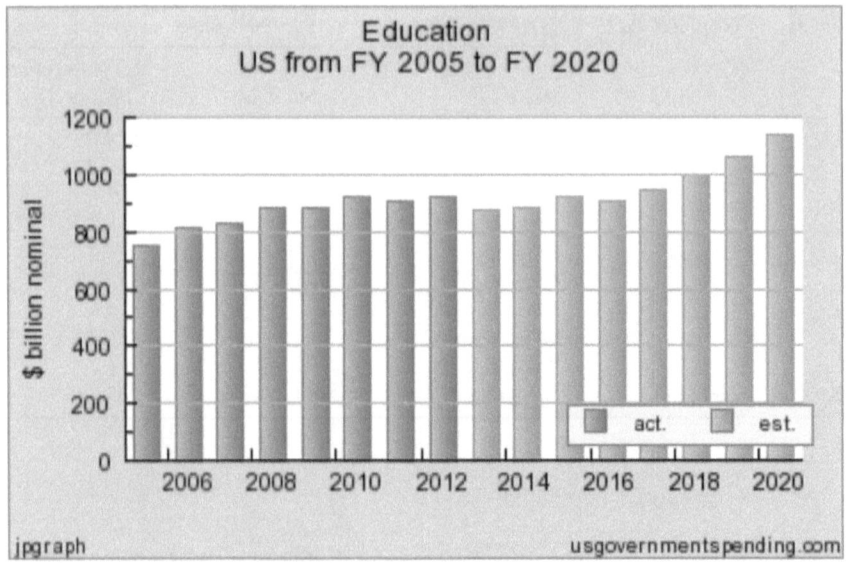

Figure 5.1. U.S. School Spending, 2005 to 2020, estimated

how the state-aid distribution formula works can help shape policies that encourage school attendance, thereby increasing funding to the school.

In summary, states are less able to support local K–12 education since the recession, as this report explains:

> At least 30 states are providing less funding per student for the 2014–15 school year than they did before the recession hit. Fourteen of these states have cut per-student funding by more than 10 percent. (These figures, like all the comparisons in this paper, are in inflation-adjusted dollars and focus on the primary form of state aid to local schools.)
>
> Most states are providing more funding per student in the new school year than they did a year ago, but funding has generally not increased enough to make up for cuts in past years. For example, Alabama is increasing school funding by $16 per pupil this year. But that is far less than is needed to offset the state's $1,144 per-pupil cut over the previous six years. (Leachman & Mai, 2014, pp. 1–2)

STATE'S ROLE IN EDUCATION

The United States has fifty states and fifty different education systems, as each state established and operates its own education system. And, education is fundamentally a state responsibility and matter, which means the schools of the United States are very different from each other under federal laws and court cases. For example, the state determines the governance systems for itself. And the differences are extreme and interesting.

For example, Hawaii has only one "school district"—and thus one state-wide school board and superintendent. This is unusual, given that Hawaii is the physically most broken-up state in the United States, with five islands separated by the Pacific Ocean. Figure 5.1 shows the state differences in school district funding (Leachman & Mai, 2014).

At the other extreme is *New Hampshire* that had $8.4 billion spent in 2014 at the *local level* and only $4.8 billion at the *state level*, with many local school districts but among the lowest state taxes and state control of education in the country. Thus, the local boards and superintends have the most authority, and the state "leaves it to the districts" to set and pay for their own programs. The remaining forty-eight states have different blends of local and state control, with overall the state having the final authority on most issues. And each state has its own balance, with Hawaii being most state centralized and New Hampshire the least state and most local controls.

Overall, then, we see the fifty states contributing $1.65 trillion total dollars to K–12 education, with the local district levels at $1.26 billion, overall in 2014. The United States thus spends about $2.9 trillion on education, not counting the federal dollars.

FEDERAL SPENDING ON EDUCATION

The federal government provided only $140 billion to education, and even that small amount is tough to analyze because of the distance from Washington to state capitals to local districts, to local schools, students, and their teachers. As Atlas explains about 2014 funding:

> Calculating that figure is challenging. Federal programs administered by the U.S. Department of Education appear in two separate parts of the federal budget, and other agencies administer large programs as well. Furthermore, measuring spending on the federal student loan program is not straightforward, and the government provides significant subsidies for higher education in the form of tax benefits.

Therefore, the $141 billion figure includes the annual appropriation for the U.S. Department of Education, spending for the U.S. Department of Education not subject to annual appropriations (i.e., mandatory spending), school meal programs administered by the U.S. Department of Agriculture, the Head

Start program in the Department of Health and Human Services, the forgone revenue and spending on education tax benefits for individuals, and military and veterans education benefits.

The federal government spent a total of $3.5 trillion in fiscal year 2013. That means the approximate $141 billion in education spending accounts for approximately 4 percent of the entire federal budget (Leachman & Mai, 2014, pp. 1–2).

Level of Funding

In 2011, Governor Jerry Brown of California advocated a shift in his state's governance system for education:

> Governor Jerry Brown's January 2011 budget proposal suggests shifting responsibility and funding for many state programs from the state to the local level. Under this "realignment" of government authority, local governments—usually counties—would be given major responsibility for providing the services in realigned programs, and the state would provide local governments with a source of funding for the new responsibilities. In addition, local governments would be granted the authority to reshape realigned programs to better accommodate local conditions and priorities. (Weston, 2011, p. 1)

Thus, the U.S. Department of Education states that the U.S. Constitution leaves the responsibility for public K–12 education primarily with the states, as explained:

> The responsibility for K-12 education rests with the states under the U.S. Constitution. There is also a compelling national interest in the quality of the nation's public schools. Therefore, the federal government, through the legislative process, provides assistance to the states and schools in an effort to supplement, not supplant, and state support. The primary source of federal K-12 support began in 1965 with the enactment of the Elementary and Secondary Education Act (ESEA).

Augenblick, Myers, and Anderson (1997) explain and compare "equity," "equitability," and "equality":

> As we define "equity" in school funding, we must also consider the companion term, "equality." Both terms have a place in our discussion, we should understand that funding can be equal, but no "equitable", since the second term means "fair." And funding all schools and students the same may not be "fair" since some students deserve and need more funding. Ensuring equity and equality or adequacy of education funding is two of the most complex problems facing state legislatures.

Not only are the concepts of equity and adequacy difficult to measure and to implement, but every state must meet the needs of a large number of school districts, which usually vary considerably in their student characteristics and needs (such as student need for compensatory or special education), costs of doing business (for example, teacher salary schedules and benefits or building and land acquisition costs), ability and willingness to raise local tax revenues, and local preferences for educational services (such as vocational training requiring expensive specialized equipment or advanced placement college-preparatory courses). (pp. 6–8)

Starting with the *Serrano v. Priest* (1971) case in California, high-poverty districts have sued for greater state aid—and greater equity. The California Supreme Court ruled (Brimley, Verstegen, and Garfield, 2012):

California's method of funding public education, because of district-to-district disparities, "fails to meet the requirements of the equal protection clause of the Fourteenth Amendment of the United States Constitution and the California Constitution." . . . . "[As] a direct result of the financing scheme they are required to pay a higher tax rate than [taxpayers] in many other school districts in order to obtain for their children the same or lesser educational opportunities afforded children in those other districts."

[That's] an actual controversy has arisen and now exists between the parties as to the validity and constitutionality of the financing scheme under the Fourteenth Amendment of the United States Constitution and under the California Constitution.

As Brimley, Verstegen, and Garfield (2012) explain, the California Supreme Court found that "the school finance system with its uneven tax burden and disparate spending patterns were unconstitutional" (p. 177). Thus, the case and following pressures reduced local (unequal) school funding from two-thirds to one-quarter, thus forcing the state to contribute more and a higher percent to education in California.

In summary, the differences between "property rich" and "property poor" districts were quite large in 1971—the year of *Serrano* decision in California—with rich districts such as Beverly Hills having $50,885 per-student property valuation, the basis of taxing, and poor districts such as Baldwin Park with only $3,706 per student, on which taxation could be made (a rich-to-poor ratio of 14 to 1).

Thus, even though residents and businesses in poor districts like Baldwin Park paid higher tax levels, they were unable to raise sufficient funds without state aid. So, even with poor district residents and business paying higher taxes on their property, the district obtained less funding, given the lower value of taxable businesses and homes (see Brimley, Verstegen, & Garfield, 2012, p. 215).

Most recently, equity groups representing the 600 Texas school districts in 2011 brought suit against the state for greater equity among districts:

> The case, *Texas Taxpayer & Student Fairness Coalition* (TTSFC) v. *State*, was filed by more than 600 Texas school districts in 2011 in response to a $5.4 billion cut in K-12 education funding by the state government. The plaintiff school districts in TTSFC educate 75 percent of the state's five million public school students. The school districts were represented by the Equity Center, the Mexican American Legal Defense and Educational Fund (MALDEF), and others.

The ruling provides a remedy to what has become a troubling pattern of denying adequate funding to low-income and minority students in states across the country. It comes on the heels of similar school funding cases in Kansas (*Gannon v. the State of Kansas*) and Washington (*McCleary v. State of Washington*) and pending cases in New York, Connecticut, and Colorado. The *Texas Taxpayer & Student Fairness Coalition* (TTSFF) ruling is especially significant because 10 percent of all public school students in the nation are enrolled in Texas schools.

Thus, each school leader—state by state, district by district, and school by school—should know the local and state funding levels, equity, and ways to secure the most local, state, and federal funding. State funding is important, yet variable; thus, leaders, particularly principals, should keep tabs on the level of school funding, district by district, and understand the levels from the federal, state and local levels.

CONCLUSION

This chapter has outlined and discussed the key roles of the state governments in funding local schools. As such, we have four recommendations for building leaders concerning this funding source:

1. Know and keep abreast of state programs and policies that will affect funding levels and programs in each school. We have shown the critical role and importance of states in supporting education. Thus, school administrators should keep in touch with their local state representatives and agencies, to be informed about state aid, whether it is basic funding or special funding for students with learning and personal problems. Local elected representatives are usually open to inquiries and requests from school leaders in their communities and districts.
2. Be responsive. But these leaders and agencies can respond only if they are informed and lobbied by educators in schools they serve. Monthly

meetings with these politicians and bureaucrats make sense: build a relationship, be supportive but be also demanding, based on the needs of schools and local kids. If they don't know, they will be unlikely to act in the best interest of their schools, leaders, teachers, and students.

3. Keep in touch with state representatives—those locally elected leaders, who can explain how new laws can benefit our schools. Work with colleagues to show interest and solidarity around key issues. If a state-aid package comes up for consideration, which local leaders like, band together and show shared force and influence, which leads to their next recommendation:

4. Let each school administrator association and union know what the school's needs are and work to influence these groups to develop influence with state governors, legislatures, and education officials. Principals have their own associations and unions, sometimes affiliated with the American Federation of School Administrators (AFSA)—and with the AFL-CIO; try to pull these large and more powerful groups into the fray: to lobby for, get, and use additional resources from the state.

Cowen and Strunk (2014) state that unions in education can matter in setting state policies, as follows:

> Focusing on unions' role in shaping education policy, we argue that collective bargaining and political organizing comprise the two central but distinct forms of influence at the district, state and national levels of decision-making. We note recent changes in state policy directly and indirectly affecting unions and union priorities. We argue that these changes may result in a variety of different conditions under which unions operate, and suggest that this variation represents fertile ground for new empirical analyses of union influence. Such work may in turn require a reconsideration of the extent of, and limitations to union power in altered educational landscapes. (p. 21)

5. Keep a close eye on the state courts, as they often handle school finance issues and cases, to avoid—where possible—making things worse—and to understand the changing legal environment of schools and education affecting one's district and schools. Finally, we realize that the local and state judicial systems play major roles play in shaping education policies. The major cases include the *Brown* decision (1954) that helped to desegregate U.S. public schools, most intensively in the South and urban school districts across the country, and the *Serrano* decision in California that started the movement to fund schools and students more equally and equitably.

Then, too, as we have discussed, state courts have often ruled in favor of greater school financial equality, by forcing the states to step in to fund high-need, lower-property wealth schools. Each school administrator should keep up with funding, per pupil, compared to other schools in other districts. More equity (fairness) often means more funding for schools, in lower-income communities. As Bruce D. Baker (2014) explained, based on the national Equity and Excellence Commission, entitled "For Each and Every Child":

> Accordingly, this commission believes the time has come for bold action by the states—and the federal government—*to redesign and reform the funding of our nation's public schools.* The deep inequities in school funding documented by another federal commission more than 40 years ago . . . remain entrenched across our nation's states and school districts at a time when more than 40 percent of all American public school children are enrolled in districts of concentrated student poverty. (U.S. Department of Education, 2013, p. 25)

REFERENCES

Augenblick, J. G., Myers, J. L., & Andersen, A. B. (1997). Equity and adequacy in school funding: The future of school funding. *Financing schools, 7*(3), 1–16.

Baker, B. D. (2014). *America's most financially disadvantaged school districts and how they got that way: How state and local governance causes school funding disparities.* Washington, DC: Center for American Progress.

Brimley, V., Verstegen, M, & Garfield, R. R. (2008). Financing education in a climate of change. NY: Allyn & Bacon.

Cowen, J., & Strunk, K. O. (2014). *How do teachers' unions influence education policy? What we know and what we need to learn.* Lansing: Michigan State University Graduate School of Education.

Kenyon, D. A. (2007, December). The property tax-school funding dilemma (policy focus report). Phoenix, AZ: Lincoln Institute of Land Policy.

Leachman, M., & Mai, C. (2014, May 20). *Most states funding schools less than before the recession.* Center of Budget and Policy Priorities.

Roth, R. W. (2015). *Public Education in Hawai'i: Past, Present & Future.* Honolulu, HA: Governor Office.

U.S. Bureau of the Census (2013). *Public school system finance,* Washington, DC: American Fact Finder.

U.S. Department of Education (2013). "For each and every child—A strategy for education equity and excellence." Washington, DC: U.S. Department of Education.

Weston, M. (2011). *Rethinking the state-local relationship: K—12 education.* Sacramento: Public Policy Institute of California.

Zeehandelaar, D., Griffith, D. et al. with David Griffith, with Joanna Smith, Michael Thier, Ross Anderson, Christine Pitts & Hovanes Gasparian (August 2015). *Schools of thought: A taxonomy of American education governance.* Washington, DC: Heartland Institute.

Chapter 6

Budgeting and Managing Federal Aid for Schools

INTRODUCTION

The federal government's role in, and financial support for, K–12 public education in the United States is relatively new and important. Traditionally, the federal government mostly left education to the states, and the states delegated the power to local school districts. This resulted in local and state governments having control over locally provided K–12 public education and providing the majority of school district funding.

This chapter explains and analyzes the following: (1) the role and importance of federal aid to U.S. education today; (2) the advantages and disadvantage of federal aid to states and local school districts; and (3) the various important programs and funding schemes, starting with the GI Bill and the Land Grant College Act for helping adults get an education in local colleges funded by the state.

Only when "national" concerns emerged around critical educational issues, often leading to legal actions—including these school issues and problems: (a) racial *segregation*, (b) the effects of school district *poverty* on children learning and lives, or (c) the *failure* of American students to compete and compare favorably with foreign students, particularly the Russians in the 1960s—did the federal government step strongly into the K–12 education policy-making arena.

Title I of the Elementary and Secondary Education Act of 1965 (ESEA), referred to now as ESSA, was signed into law in December 2015 by President Obama and has several programs, including the following:

Title I: Improving the Academic Achievement of the Disadvantaged

—Part A: Improving the Academic Achievement of the Disadvantaged
—Part B: Reading First
—Part C: Migrant and Bilingual Education
—Part D: Institutional Education

Thus, ESSA helps the poorer schools with racial desegregation and national productivity and is an important example of federal interest and involvement in education and its key roles in local schools and districts. ESSA helped Title I become clearer and more focused.

The purpose of Title I is to ensure that all children have a fair, equal, and significant opportunity to obtain a high-quality education and reach, at a minimum, proficiency on challenging state academic achievement standards and state academic assessments. This purpose can be accomplished by the following twelve efforts.

1. Ensuring that high-quality academic assessments, accountability systems, teacher preparation and training, curriculum, and instructional materials are aligned with challenging state academic standards so that students, teachers, parents, and administrators can measure progress against common expectations for student academic achievement
2. Meeting the educational needs of low-achieving children in our nation's highest-poverty schools, limited English proficient children, migratory children, children with disabilities, Indian children, neglected or delinquent children, and young children in need of reading assistance
3. Closing the achievement gap between high- and low-performing children, especially the achievement gaps between minority and nonminority students, and between disadvantaged children and their more advantaged peers
4. Holding schools, local educational agencies, and states accountable for improving the academic achievement of all students, and identifying and turning around low-performing schools that have failed to provide a high-quality education to their students, while providing alternatives to students in such schools to enable the students to receive a high-quality education
5. Distributing and targeting resources sufficiently to make a difference to local educational agencies and schools where needs are greatest
6. Improving and strengthening accountability, teaching, and learning by using state assessment systems designed to ensure that students are meeting challenging State academic achievement and content standards and increasing achievement overall, but especially for the disadvantaged
7. Providing greater decision-making authority and flexibility to schools and teachers in exchange for greater responsibility for student performance

8. Providing children an enriched and accelerated educational program, including the use of school-wide programs or additional services that increase the amount and quality of instructional time
9. Promoting school-wide reform and ensuring the access of children to effective scientifically based instructional strategies and challenging academic content
10. Significantly elevating the quality of instruction by providing staff in participating schools with substantial opportunities for professional development
11. Coordinating services under all parts of this title with each other, with other educational services, and, to the extent feasible, with other agencies providing services to youth, children, and families
12. Affording parents substantial and meaningful opportunities to participate in the education of their children

School principals should come to understand the roles, potential, and limitations of the federal funding and involvement in supporting local schools. For as the U.S. Department of Education explains, "Education is primarily a State and local responsibility in the United States . . . with only about 12-plus percent Federal funds." And the federal role and influence came late as well, in several areas. The antipoverty and civil rights laws of the 1960s and 1970s brought about a dramatic emergence of the U.S. Education Department's equal access mission, including the following:

- The passage of laws such as Title VI of the Civil Rights Act of 1964, Title IX of the Education Amendments of 1972, and Section 504 of the Rehabilitation Act of 1973 which prohibited discrimination based on race, sex, and disability, respectively, made civil rights enforcement a fundamental and long-lasting focus of the Department of Education.
- In 1965, the ESEA launched a comprehensive set of programs, including the Title I program of federal aid to disadvantaged children to address the problems of poor urban and rural areas. And in that same year, the Higher Education Act authorized assistance for postsecondary education, including financial aid programs for needy college students.

For example, before the mid-1950s, school racial segregation was common nationwide, but especially in the South. Hence, with the U.S. Supreme Court taking action on May 17, 1954, in the *Brown v. Board of Education,* the federal government worked to "desegregate" America's schools and undo the "separate but equal" approach to education, which meant racial separation. As court determined, after the five cases were heard together by the Court in December 1952, the outcome remained uncertain. The Court ordered the parties to answer a series of questions about the specific intent of the congressmen and senators who framed the Fourteenth Amendment to the U.S. Constitution, and about the Court's power to dismantle segregation.

The Court then scheduled another oral argument in December 1953. Wrapping up his presentation to the Court in that second hearing, Justice Thurgood Marshall emphasized that segregation was rooted in the desire to keep "the people who were formerly in slavery as near to that stage as is possible." Even with such powerful arguments from Thurgood Marshall and other LDF attorneys, it took another five months for the newly appointed Chief Justice Earl Warren's behind-the-scenes lobbying to yield a unanimous decision.

School District Spending Equity

Similarly, about two decades later, in the California's courts, families sought for the state to provide greater financial equity, and sued in *Serrano v. Priest* (1971) for greater financial equity among school districts, regardless of local real estate property values and wealth equity. As explained by McDonnell (2015),

> Initiated in 1968 in the Superior Court of Los Angeles County, *Serrano v. Priest* (John Serrano was a parent of one of several Los Angeles public school students; Ivy Baker Priest was the California State Treasurer at the time and a former US Treasurer) set forth three causes of action (quotes from the decision).
>
> California's method of funding public education, because of district-to-district disparities, "fails to meet the requirements of the equal protection clause of the Fourteenth Amendment of the United States Constitution and the California Constitution." (p. 2)

America spent over $550 billion a year on public elementary and secondary education in 2015—and up to $597 billion in 2016—although the distribution of funds, which is often based on local property values and taxes, is sometimes unfair and inequitable without the federal government playing a larger role to remove funding disparities.

As shown in table 6.1, about $76 billion is *federal*, while *state* funding is almost $260 billion, and *local* contribution is slightly more at nearly $262 billion, with the total almost $600 billion (totaling $597,485,869,000).

Table 6.1. Spending on Public Schools, K–12, in 2016 School Year

TOTAL FUNDING OF U.S. PUBLIC EDUCATION in 2016: $597,485,869,000	
1—Federal:	$75.99 billion (12.7% of total)
2—State:	$259.8 billion (43.5% of total)
3—Local:	$261.7 billion (43.8% of total) wealth and income
Total:	$597,485,869,000 (approx. $600 billion)

And during the so-called War on Poverty, the federal government worked with states and localities to end poverty, in large part, by starting to invest in and improve schools. Thus, this chapter aims to present the key, critical role and limitations of the federal government in working with the fifty states, DC, and the approximately 13,000-plus local school systems; and the public and private school efforts of leadership to tackle major problems, such as literacy, poverty, and future employment for students, in K–12 schools. This chapter will treat these issues, all around the federal role, responsibility, and impact on local and state K–12 schools and education:

1. Legal Roles and Actions: Perhaps the best way to start this analysis is to examine the federal court actions in education that affected local schools and their funding. The *Brown* (1955) decision worked to end racial segregation in U.S. schools and to "integrate" all children into the previously all-white schools.

Not easy. As explained, the unanimous Court wrote that a quality education was crucial for all children and ruled that it was the state's responsibility to ensure educational equality. The Leadership Conference, "the nation's premier civil & human rights coalition," explains the importance of the *Brown* decision as follows:

> Today, education is perhaps the most important function of state and local governments. Compulsory school attendance laws and the great expenditures for education both demonstrate our recognition of the importance of education to our democratic society. It is required in the performance of our most basic public responsibilities, even service in the armed forces. It is the very foundation of good citizenship.
> Today, it is a principal instrument in awakening the child to cultural values, in preparing him for later professional training, and in helping him to adjust normally to his environment. In these days, it is doubtful that any child may reasonably be expected to succeed in life if he is denied the opportunity of an education. Such an opportunity, where the state has undertaken to provide it, is a right that must be made available to all on equal terms. (Coffin & Cooper, 2017, p. *viii*)

2. Federal Efforts and Programs: Next, we shall present information on federal programs, usually from the U.S. Department of Education, to meet special needs and difficulties that have triggered national programs such as ESEA and, more recently, ESSA. Each principal should know and use these programs to help students with needs and disabilities in their schools and districts.
3. National and State Standards—and Local Needs and Expectations: Finally, school leaders should become aware of what they need to do to

meet expectations and school finances, from all levels: (a) local boards and communities and, of course, local superintendents, school board, communities, and even local teacher associations and unions; (b) state education departments and other state regulators and regulations; and (c) federal laws, policies, and programs that may benefit children in their schools.

Pushing Funds down to Teacher and Students in Classrooms

School leaders should be aware of how much funding, and "dollars-per-pupil" reach the classrooms in their schools. Cooper, Fusarelli, Randall (2004) built a model for tracking dollars to the kids in the classroom. The *resource cost model,* which Chambers recommends, "places paramount importance on measuring productivity and the cost-effectiveness analysis, the economist's stock in trade" (Cooper, Fusarelli, Randall, 2004).

Several states, including Hawaii, South Carolina, and Rhode Island, have adopted another reporting tool that integrates with the existing GAAP accounting systems utilized at the school and district levels. This financial analysis model allows expenditure data to be reported on a school-by-school basis—and actually tracks dollars spent in the classroom for "classroom instruction." The reporting program allows policy-makers to "explore the equity, efficiency, and effectiveness of spending" (Cooper, Nisonoff, & Speakman, 2001, p. 28) between *schools* as opposed to school districts.

Moving resources in education into the classroom can often mean more and better teachers, equipment, materials, books, and opportunities. Hawaii is a case in point, along with South Carolina, where working for Hawaii's governor Linda Lingle, we tracked dollars from the state through the local school systems to the school and classroom—and to the child.

Points of Interest and Importance

This section of the chapter examines key areas in which (1) the federal government funding may reach and improve individual schools and (2) how these dollars arrive, should and must be used, and what we can learn from these four cases.

Case 1: Title I and Other ESSA Funding for Poor Children: The federal government, while highly visible, is usually concentrated on certain key national issues. The main one for more than a half century was racial and SES (socioeconomic status) equity so that children regardless of their family's race, background, income, and location could and would receive a quality education. The major federal program is ESEA that became Every Student Succeeds Act (ESSA). Note that President Obama signed the program into law, as one of his major accomplishments in education:

President Obama signed the Every Student Succeeds Act (ESSA) into law on December 10, 2015. ESSA includes provisions that will help to ensure success for students and schools. The following are just a few qualities of the law:

- Advances equity by upholding critical protections for America's disadvantaged and high-need students.
- Requires—for the first time—that all students in America be taught to high academic standards that will prepare them to succeed in college and careers.
- Ensures that vital information is provided to educators, families, students, and communities through annual statewide assessments that measure students' progress toward those high standards.
- Helps to support and grow local innovations—including evidence-based and placed interventions developed by local leaders and educators—consistent with our Investing in Innovation and Promise Neighborhoods
- Sustains and expands this administration's historic investments in increasing access to high-quality preschool.
- Maintains an expectation that accountability and action will cause positive change in our lowest-performing schools, where groups of students are not making progress, and where graduation rates are low over extended time. The Elementary and Secondary Education Act (ESEA) was signed into law in 1965 by President Lyndon Johnson, who believed that "full educational opportunity" should be "our first national goal." From its inception, ESEA was a civil rights law to offer quality education to all in education, regardless of students' race or background.

ESEA offered new grants to districts serving low-income students, federal grants for textbooks and library books, funding for special education centers, and scholarships for low-income college students. Additionally, the law provided federal grants to state educational agencies to improve the quality of elementary and secondary education in their jurisdictions.

NO CHILD LEFT BEHIND (2002): NCLB AND ACCOUNTABILITY

No Child Left Behind (NCLB) put in place measures that exposed achievement gaps among traditionally underserved students, and their peers, and spurred an important national dialogue on education improvement. This focus on accountability has been critical in ensuring a quality education for all children, yet also revealed challenges in the effective implementation of this goal. Parents, educators, and elected officials across the country recognized that a strong, updated law was necessary to expand opportunity to all students; support schools, teachers, and principals; and strengthen our education system and economy.

In 2012, the Obama administration began granting flexibility to states regarding specific requirements of NCLB in exchange for rigorous and comprehensive state-developed plans designed to close achievement gaps.

Soon, the U.S. Department of Education will work with states and districts to begin implementing the new law. The NCLB is in the same tradition as ESEA to help poor children do better in school. As the purpose of the law explains (Klein, 2002),

> The No Child Left Behind law—the 2002 update of the Elementary and Secondary Education Act—effectively scaled up the federal role in holding schools accountable for student outcomes.
>
> It was the product of a collaboration between civil rights and business groups—as well as both Democrats and Republicans on Capitol Hill and the Bush administration—which sought to advance American competitiveness and close the achievement gap between poor and minority students and their more advantaged peers. Since 2002, it's had an outsized impact on teaching, learning, and school improvement—and become increasingly controversial with educators and the general public. (p. 1)

Case 2: Special Education Funding for Special Needs and Disabled Children: once the federal government worked to handle some of the problems of race and social class (SES—socioeconomic status) in education, to help black, minority, and poor children to get a good education, the next issue were children with disabilities. First passed in 1975, the federal law was recently renewed as IDEA (Individuals with Disabilities Act). Here's a brief history and background on the 1975 law with renewals? As Bishop (2013) explains,

> The topic of federal funding has been a concern since PL 94–142 (the Education of All Handicapped Children Act, now the Individuals with Disabilities Education Act or IDEA) was passed in 1975. Within this law was a promise of major funding for special education: this legislation mandated that 40 percent of all special education funding would be provided by the federal government.
>
> While this level of federal funding is still the expressed goal of many, in reality, this funding has not exceeded 17 percent and typically is closer to 11 to 12 percent. This issue became more of a concern when the recent congressional sequestration went into effect and 9.1 percent was taken from the top of all federal funding, including education for children with disabilities. (pp. 1–2)

Case 3: Federal Help with STEM (Science, Technology, Engineering, and Science) in Schools: the federal government agencies have long been concerned about quality of teaching math, science, and technology in our schools. For the nation's economic standing and defense depend in part on students' learning STEM skills, as well as improving manufacturing and life.

For as President Obama explained in March 2015, "[Science] is more than a school subject, or the periodic table, or the properties of waves. It is an approach to the world—a critical way to understand and explore and engage with the world—and then have the capacity to change that world."

President Barack Obama, on March 23, 2015, further explained,

> The United States has developed as a global leader, in large part, through the genius and hard work of its scientists, engineers, and innovators. In a world that's becoming increasingly complex, where success is driven not only by *what* you know, but by what you *can do* with what you know, it's more important than ever for our youth to be equipped with the knowledge and skills to solve tough problems, gather and evaluate evidence, and make sense of information. These are the types of skills that students learn by studying science, technology, engineering, and math—subjects collectively known as STEM.

So as a rule, each school leaders should follow federal funding for STEM, as it comes down the pipe or off the computer.

Case 4: Special Federal Funding for Schools: The federal role and financial support for K–12 public education in the United States are both fairly new and very complex. For previously, the fed's mostly left education to each state and local school districts, which meant that we had mainly local and state funding and control of education.

Only when "national" concerns emerged around critical issues—including school racial segregation, the effects of school district poverty, and/or the failure of American students to compete with foreign kids, particularly the Russian Communists in the 1960s in the sciences—did the federal government (i.e., the president, Congress, and U.S. Department of Education) step into K–12 educational policy-making, nationwide with important effects on school finance.

Title I of ESEA for the poor, racial desegregation for black kids and Latinos/as, and national productivity are three important examples of the federal interest in education and their key roles in local schools and districts. Principals should come to understand the roles, potential, and limitations of the federal involvement in funding local schools.

For as the U.S. Department of Education explains, "Education is primarily a State and local responsibility in the United States . . . with only about 11 percent Federal funding." And the role and influence came late as well, in several areas.

The antipoverty and civil rights laws of the 1960s and 1970s brought about a dramatic emergence of the department's equal access mission.

- The passage of laws such as Title VI of the Civil Rights Act of 1964, Title IX of the Education Amendments of 1972, and Section 504 of the Rehabilitation Act of 1973 that prohibited discrimination based on race, sex, and disabilities, respectively, made civil rights enforcement a fundamental and long-lasting focus of the Department of Education.

- In 1965, the Elementary and Secondary Education Act (ESEA) launched a comprehensive set of programs, including the Title I program of federal aid to disadvantaged children, to address the problems of poor urban and rural areas. And in that same year, the Higher Education Act authorized assistance for postsecondary education, with financial aid programs for needy college students.
- For example, before the mid-1950s, school racial segregation was common in the South and other areas of the nation. So, with the U.S. Supreme Court taking action on May 17, 1954, in the *Brown v. Board of Education,* the federal government worked to "desegregate" America's schools. Similarly, about two decades later. The *Serrano v. Priest* (1971) suit sought financial equity among school districts. Regardless of local real property values and wealth equity. As explained,

> Initiated in 1968 in the Superior Court of Los Angeles County, *Serrano v. Priest* (John Serrano was a parent of one of several Los Angeles public school students; Ivy Baker Priest was the California State Treasurer at the time) set forth three causes of action (quotes from the decision).
>
> California's method of funding public education, because of district-to-district disparities, "fails to meet the requirements of the equal protection clause of the Fourteenth Amendment of the United States Constitution and the California Constitution."

America spent over $550 billion a year on public elementary and secondary education in 2015—and up to $597 billion in 2016—although the distribution of funds is often based on local property and property tax and is often not fair or equitable, as shown in table 6.2.

And during the so-called War on Poverty, the federal government worked with states and localities to end poverty, in large part, by improving local school.

Thus, this chapter presents the key, critical role of the federal government in working with the fifty states, Washington, DC, and the approximately 14,000 local school systems and the public and private school leadership to tackle major problems, such as literacy, poverty, and future employment for students, while in K–12 schools.

Table 6.2. Spending on Public Schools, K–12, in 2016 School Year

TOTAL FUNDING OF U.S. PUBLIC EDUCATION in 2016: $597,485,869,000	
Federal:	$75.99 billion (12.7% of total)
State:	$259.8 billion (43.5% of total)
Local:	$261.7 billion (43.8% of total) wealth and income.

3. Legal Role and Actions: Perhaps the best way to start is to examine the federal court actions in education that affect local schools and their funding.
4. Federal Efforts and Programs: Next, we shall present information of federal programs, usually from the U.S. Department of Education, to meet special needs and difficulties that have triggered national programs such as ESEA and recently ESSA. Each principal should know and use these programs to help students with needs and disabilities in their schools and districts.
5. National and State Standards—and Local Needs and Expectations: Finally, school leaders should become aware of what they need to do to meet expectations and school finances, from all levels: (a) local boards and communities and of course, local superintendents, school board, communities, and even local teacher associations and unions; (b) state departments and other state regulators and regulations; and (c) federal laws, policies, and programs that may benefit children in their schools.

SPECIAL SPENDING FOR CHILDREN WITH SPECIAL NEEDS

The Individuals with Disabilities Education Act (IDEA) is the chief legislative and mandated program of and service driver for special education in the nation. However, IDEA has been underfunded since its inception in 1975. Although President Obama promised full funding of IDEA, he did not seek or produced full funding during his terms in office. The president's FY-2017 budget will fund IDEA at FY-2016 levels of only 16 percent of the full cost of all IDEA special education mandated programs and services.

The underfunding IDEA (at only 16 percent) is less than half of the federal government's original 40 percent limit on funding students with educational and physiological disabilities. Moreover, the federal government promised to pay only 40 percent of the national average per-special education pupil expenditure, penalizing districts with higher than average per-pupil special education expenditures.

The highest funding level provided by the federal government for funding IDEA's mandated programs and services was 18 percent in 2005. This means that President Obama's proposed funding level for FY-2017 is below that of more than a decade ago under President Bush.

Funding IDEA at only 16 percent means that 84 percent must be paid for by public school districts themselves, nationwide, because the IDEA's programs and services are mandated. These programs and services require that any funding deficit be paid for by the local public school districts themselves.

Therefore, the underfunding of IDEA requires districts to make up for the dollar shortfall by cutting nonmandate-protected programs and services.

Hence, the underfunding of IDEA is one of the most powerful drivers of public school district budget cuts nationwide. Moreover, the chronic underfunding of IDEA and the budget cuts it fosters often pit regular and special education parents, students, and teachers against one another in a battle for scarce financial, material, and human educational resources.

> Question: Should not the federal government be required to pay 100 percent of its special education mandates?
>
> Answer: Special education expenses are one of the fastest growing financial challenges confronting local school districts nationwide—and particularly in New Jersey. School districts throughout New Jersey pay not only all of the general expense for their special education students but also the majority of the "excess cost" of special education, defined as the per-pupil cost of special education that exceeds the regular student cost.

Declining state and federal aid not only has increased the proportion of property taxes used to fund schools, but has also heightened the pressure to find necessary resources perhaps by reducing programs and services for regular education students in order to fund mandate-protected programs and services such as special education.

Special education costs are driven primarily by expensive out-of-district placements, mandated preschool programs, including intensive services for autistic students, and lower special education student to staff ratios—as well as by parents suing school districts to obtain private school placements for their children. The legal fees for such lawsuits account for another escalating expense for schools.

In addition, if a school district loses in a New Jersey administrative court, the district not only has to pay for the judgment costs but also all of the plaintiff's legal costs regardless of the length of the trial. It seems as if holding New Jersey school districts harmless from such lawsuits would be another way in which to enable school districts to allocate more of their scarce resources to instruction.

Many districts find that out-of-district placements can consume as much as 50 percent of their special education budget. The students placed in out-of-district schools tend to be the most expensive because they are usually the ones most in need of special education programs and services. Depending on the student's disability, the annual cost of sending a student to an out-of-district private school can range from roughly $60,000 to over $250,000—especially for the most educationally and physically challenged students.

The federal government forces its traditional public schools to pay for an ever-increasing proportion of special education costs by underfunding IDEA mandates, forcing districts to increase local property taxes, and identify funds to offset the shortfall through means that adversely affect the regular education budget. Underfunded IDEA mandates can result in much larger class sizes as school districts are forced to consider reducing the numbers of regular education teachers and aides. Larger class sizes often lead to lower test scores that make it more difficult for students, schools, and districts to achieve academic progress and control costs.

Unless public school districts, nationwide, not only wish to avoid IDEA-driven budget cuts to offset IDEA's underfunding and a downward spiral in the quality of education stemming from IDEA's underfunding but also continued higher property taxes, then the districts nationwide should band together and demand the federal government fund IDEA 100 percent, and, therefore, pay for all of the costs of IDEA's mandated programs and services.

Moreover, full funding of IDEA would prevent the budget cuts it currently fosters. Stopping IDEA-driven budget cuts would end the conflict among regular and special education parents, students, and teachers over scarce financial, material, and human educational resources, and put the focus on working together to provide a quality education for all.

POINTS OF INTEREST AND IMPORTANCE

This section of the chapter examines four key areas in which the federal government's funding may reach and improve individual schools and their students. And we examine just how these dollars arrive, should and must be used to improve schools and their students' learning—and what we can learn from these four cases.

CASE 1: SPECIAL FEDERAL FUNDING FOR HIGHER EDUCATION IN THE UNITED STATES

The Land Grant College Act and GI Bill

In the history of the United States, two federal funding programs stand out. In 1865, Congress passed the Land Grant College Act, which distributed thousands of acres of federal land to the states to open "agricultural and technical colleges" (A&T, or "ag-tech"). Some states sold the former federal land and made use of the funds to open and build new ag-tech colleges all across the country; other states opened colleges on the land grant acres.

Virtually every state now has important ag-tech colleges for teaching agriculture and engineering. New York has Cornell University, for example, that is partially land grant public and part private, with most of the professional and technical schools remaining public, and the undergraduate Cornell College is private.

The other important federal program was the GI Bill, passed at the end of World War II (1944) to educate the millions of men and women who had sacrificed their education and sometimes their lives and served in the military. Millions have financed their higher education using funds from the GI Bill. President Roosevelt brought the law into action as follows:

> On June 22, 1944, President Franklin D. Roosevelt signed the Servicemen's Readjustment Act, better known as the G.I. Bill. Fearing the consequences of millions of veterans returning from war to scarce employment and few housing opportunities, Roosevelt passed the legislation to offer unemployment compensation, home and business loans and tuition support.

CONCLUSION

Thus, when the federal government thinks big, the results are often commensurately big; and the bigger the problem, the bigger the solution at the national level. The federal government can create its own program in education or fund the local and states' efforts. Either way, every level can benefit. And the bill was called the GI Bill of Rights:

> The initials "GI" originally stood for anything of "government issue." Eventually, they came to designate an enlisted soldier in the U. S. armed forces. In 1944 Congress passed the Servicemen's Readjustment Act, the so-called GI Bill of Rights, which provided government aid (a) for veterans' hospitals and vocational rehabilitation; (b) for the purchase by veterans of houses, farms, and businesses; and (c) for four years of college education for veterans. Later, the act extended to veterans of the Korean War. The Readjustment Benefits Act of 1966 gave similar rights to all veterans of service in the U. S. armed forces, whether during wartime or peacetime. Subsequent acts provided for additional benefits. With the abolition of the draft in 1973, benefits were tied to length of service. (Berman, 2015, p. 1)

Therefore, the federal government and its policies are remote from most American school children—their schools, teachers, and families. But the federal government plays an important role, setting legal policies and precedents, and is often in a position to influence the schools by offering advice, funding, and legal remedies. Or, as one agency explained, during the past half-century, federal education policy has played an increasingly critical role in determining what happens in American classrooms—and ultimately in the minds and hearts of American students.

Thus, administrators in our schools need to be aware, keep pace, and live by the federal requirement, as best they can, as the Southern Education Research Board (2012) explains:

> As a result, despite federal mandates, state interventions and system expenditures of millions of dollars earmarked for reform, many school districts serving high-needs students have a substantial percentage of schools not meeting Adequate Yearly Progress (AYP) goals under the federal *No Child Left Behind Act*. (p. 20)

REFERENCES

Berman, E. (2015). How the G.I. Bill changed the face of higher education in America. *TIME*. Retrieved from http://time.com/3915231/student-veterans/.

Bishop, N. (2013, August 21). What do federal budget cuts really mean for public school special education programs? *Special Education Guide*. Retrieved from http://www.specialeducationguide.com/blog/what-do-federal-budget-cuts-really-mean-for-public-school-special-education-programs/.

Coffin, S. V., & Cooper, B. S. (Eds.) (2017). Sound school finance for Educational Excellence. Lanham, MD: Rowman & Littlefield.

Cooper, B. S., Fusarelli, L. D. & Randall, E. V. (2004). Better policies, better schools: theories and applications. NY: Allyn & Bacon.

Cooper, B. S., Nisonoff, P. H., & Speakman, S. T. (2001). Advanced budget technology in education: The future is now. *School Business Affairs, 67*(2), 27–32.

Klein, A. (2002). No Child Left Behind: An overview. Retrieved from http://www.edweek.org/ew/section/multimedia/no-child-left-behind-overview-definition-summary.html.

McDonnell, L. M. (2005). No Child Left Behind and the federal role in education: Evolution or revolution? *Peabody Journal of Education, 80*(2), 19–38.

Southern Education Research Board (2012). *Federal education policy and the states, 1945–2009: A brief synopsis*. Albany: The New York State Department of Education.

Chapter 7

Budgeting and Managing Local Revenues

INTRODUCTION

One of the defining characteristics of American public schools is their importance, local control and, yes, local funding. Local dollars mostly come from local property taxes that provide the majority of funding for most of districts, nationwide. Homes, property, and businesses provide what funds for local schools and children?

(Thought starter question: What are examples of local school funding in one's district, town, county, or community and in what amounts and for what purposes or programs and for which kids?)

While state and federal governments contribute additional, significant funding in most states—Hawaii is an exception with no local districts—are locally funded and managed. This localism means that the community and the school boards, superintendents, and principals have a strong voice in the control and management of our local public schools and their funding. As the National School Boards Association (NSBA, 2014) explained,

> The most important responsibility of school boards is to work with their communities to improve student achievement in their local public schools. School boards derive their power and authority from the state. In compliance with state and federal laws, school boards establish policies and regulations by which their local schools are governed. (See more https://www.nsba.org/about-us/ frequently-asked-questions#sthash. 9KQci Uyc.dpuf, 2001.)

This chapter explains and explores the key role of the states in funding and supporting and regulating local districts and schools. Within the fifty states, as explained by the 2012 Census of Governments, the U.S. Census Bureau enumerated the following numbers of school systems in the county: 13,506 school district governments in the fifty states. Thus, we shall explore and explain the local nature, control, and funding, of American public (and some private) schools, including the advantages and disadvantages of local funding—and control—of our schools.

Advantages of Local Control and Funding

Both local control and funding of public schools have certain major advantages. First, the teachers, principals, and parents have a greater voice in local education, with less statewide and national influence. After all, school boards are basic, local *democratic institutions that* represent their educators, families, and stakeholders of their own local communities. The American Legislative Exchange Council (ALEC) explains the role of local school boards as follows:

> The Innovation Schools and School Districts Act creates a mechanism for schools, groups of schools, and districts to adopt plans that try new ways of delivering instruction and/or allocating resources. It creates a new classification of school districts, "Districts of Innovation," that have one or more schools implementing these plans. Districts of innovation are provided a greater degree of autonomy and can waive some statutory requirements. (Coffin & Cooper, 2017, p. 18)

Second, teachers can form important local spokes-groups for their schools and classrooms, because most states have laws that allow local "collective bargaining" and union activity. This "voice" is particularly important in the larger, urban districts where teachers need someone to speak for their needs in the classroom in teaching their subjects and in receiving decent pay and benefits (e.g., health care, tenure, benefits, and pensions).

While most states allow a collective voice through unionization and collective bargaining, some still do not. And American teachers do not "speak" with one union voice, since the United Federation of Teachers (UFT) and the larger National Education Association (NEA) were not able to agree to merge (see Cooper, 1998); the two unions speak up when teachers need them (Fusarelli & Cooper, 1999), but a merger was rejected by the NEA in New Orleans in 1998.

For example, the NEA explained its role and position on local school policies and programs, as follows:

> That effort received a big boost last week in Washington, DC, when the country's largest union, the National Education Association (NEA), voted at its national convention to support the Portland resolution and to encourage state and local affiliates to create and promote climate literacy resolutions in their

own communities, using the Portland resolution as a model. The NEA has close to 3 million members, and its convention is dubbed "the world's largest deliberative assembly," with 7,000 delegates. (Bigelow, 2016, n.p.)

Even in the 2016 presidential election, candidates spoke and argued over local education and funding, and the NEA supported the Democratic candidate, Hillary R. Clinton, who explained her relationship with teachers:

> The NEA enthusiastically responded to Hillary's bridge building, and it heard her promise to do what teachers want the most from officeholders. We want to be partners. We want to be re-invited by a president to our "seat at the table." We want a president—not just a presidential candidate—who says and believes, "I have this old-fashioned idea that when we are making decisions about education, we actually should listen to our educators." (Thompson, 2016, p. 2)

And Donald J. Trump had his own view of school spending, as he explained just before his presidential campaign:

> "We spend more per student than any other nation."
>
> *Education spending:* "People are tired of spending more money on education than any nation in the world per capita."
>
> *Local control of education:* "Education has to be local."
>
> *American education in an international context:* "We're 26th in the world. 25 countries are better than us at education. And some of them are like third world countries. But we're becoming a third world country." (White, 2015, pp. 22–23)

Equity among School Districts' Spending on Education

A second critical issue involving local control and funding of our public schools is the lack of district spending equity, often based on differences in local residential and business property wealth, among districts in the same state and region. Much like the desegregation efforts in the 1950s following the *Brown v. Board of Education of Topeka, Kansas* (1955), school funding inequalities court cases began about seventeen years later, with the California case, *Serrano vs. Priest* (California Supreme Court: *Serrano v. Priest*, 5 Cal.3d 584, 1971).

The issue: As local "property values" differ, poorer school districts have problems trying to raise sufficient funds for their schools, and they turn to the state for funding. As the case came to explain, initiated in 1968 in the Superior Court of Los Angeles County, *Serrano v. Priest* (John Serrano was a parent of one of several Los Angeles public school students; Ivy Baker Priest was the California State Treasurer at the time and former U.S. Treasurer) set forth three causes of action (quotes from the decision).

California's method of funding public education, because of district-to-district disparities, "fails to meet the requirements of the equal protection clause of the Fourteenth Amendment of the United States Constitution and the California Constitution."

> [As] a direct result of the financing scheme they are required to pay a higher tax rate than [taxpayers] in many other school districts in order to obtain for their children the same or lesser educational opportunities afforded children in those other districts.
>
> [That] an actual controversy has arisen and now exists between the parties as to the validity and constitutionality of the financing scheme under the Fourteenth Amendment of the United States Constitution and under the California Constitution.
>
> The Court agreed with the plaintiffs, largely on equal-protection grounds, and returned the case to the trial court for further proceedings.

In the end, the *Serrano* decision in California—and similar cases in other states—ruled that local districts are often fiscally inequitable based on property tax–based funding, since local property wealth and tax value vary greatly from district to district, and that the state has a legal responsibility in many states to help equalize local spending by subsidizing local funding. One explanation of the effects of *Serrano* in California and in similar cases in other states:

> After *Serrano* I, the Legislature enacted SB90, which established a "squeeze formula" to begin a leveling of recurring school-district income based on the average daily attendance revenue limit. The Superior Court in *Serrano* ruled in 1974 that, although SB90 was a step in the right direction, "wealth-related disparities" were still impermissible. *Serrano* II affirmed the trial court's judgment, giving the state six years to bring the system into compliance. (Coffin & Cooper, 2017, p. 18)

And the courts moved to create greater equity and equality of per-pupil spending for districts with poor local property wealth—and thus lower-property tax income for their schools. As the courts determined,

> Thus, in 1968–69, the Baldwin Park School District spent $577.49 to educate each of its pupils, while Pasadena spent $840.19 per pupil and Beverly Hills spent $1,231.72 per public. This "economic chasm" between various districts with respect to tax base and expenditures meant "poorer" districts had to tax

themselves at much higher rates to match the expenditures of wealthier districts, if this was even possible.

As the Supreme Court put it, "affluent districts can have their cake and eat it too; they can provide a high quality education for their children while paying lower taxes. Poor districts, by contrast, have no cake at all." (See more at: http://corporate.findlaw.com/law-library/separate-and-unequal-serrano-played-an-important-role-in.html#sthash.6 Of 9 Nov.puf, 2001, p. 11.)

Equity is the major issue across districts in the states, based on property wealth and taxation. As was shown in the *Serrano v. Priest* case in California and later in other states, the issue remains important as follows:

> The statistics recited in *Serrano* I were provocative. Recurring public-school funds came primarily from local district taxes on real property (55.7 percent) and State School Fund aid (35.5 percent). The Legislature authorized each county to levy taxes on real property within a school district at a rate needed to meet the district's annual education budget. (See more at: http://corporate.findlaw.com/law-library/separate-and-unequal-serrano-played-an-important-role-in.html#sthash.6Of9oveN.dpuf.)

How Many Dollars Are Really Reaching Students in the Classroom?

The next issue gets even closer to teachers and their students in the class: *How much money in each district and school reaches the child in the classroom*. In 1973, Bruce S. Cooper and Sheree T. Speakman at Coopers & Lybrand accounting firm built a model called the *Financial Analysis Model (FAM)* or *In$ite*, for tracking dollars from the central district office to the school and to the classroom.

FAM (or *In$ite*) was developed for New York City's Mayor Rudy Giuliani since New York City spent millions on education but was having trouble producing well-educated, high-testing students who could graduate high school. As one description explains,

> This proposal's signatories call on policymakers to transform the school funding system in service of meeting our high ambitions for student learning. We envision a transparent system in which:
>
> - Funding from all levels follows every student to whichever public school he or she attends;
> - The amount varies according to the student's needs;
> - Funding arrives at schools a real dollars that can be spent flexibly, with accountability gauged results rather than inputs, programs, or activities.

The FAM model is still being used by districts across the country to increase and improve the use of funding, by driving the resources to the actual teacher in the actual classroom, where the students are being taught and are learning. If a high amount of resources are spent on "overhead," administration, and other nonpedagogical purposes, the kids and their teachers can suffer. Poverty begins at home and carries over to the classroom in poor communities and schools.

Budgeting and budget analysis are important activities and points of analysis. William Hartman (1999) has dissected and analyzed models of budgeting that can help each school leader to improve the results and uses of budgeting and funding.

Types of Operating Budgets:

1. Line-item budgeting: Mundt, Oslen, and Steinberg (1982) define line item, or traditional budgeting, as "a technique in which line items, or objects of expenditures—for example, personnel, supplies, contractual services, and capital outlays—are the focus of analysis, authorization, and control" (p. 36).

While helpful in tracking costs, line-item budgeting is virtually useless for planning or management, because the functions of the expenditures are not explained and the particular need, school site, and type of students being served are lost in spending aggregated by "line." Thus, *teachers' salaries,* for example, are a budget line item, but which teachers, at which schools, teaching which types of students (e.g., bilingual special needs, ELL, ESL) is neither given nor explained.

2. Function/object budgeting: Most districts use function/object budgeting, because it organizes spending around the basic *functions* of the system, such as instruction, student support, operations, administration, and transportation. In addition, functions are subdivided (e.g., into elementary instruction, middle school instruction, high school instruction), while the objects being purchased (e.g., elementary textbooks, middle school windows, high school cleaning equipment) are also specified. Personnel services and salaries with benefits may be handled by function, that is, for instructional, support, or plant maintenance staff, for example.

Although these broad categories, objects, and processes are generally the same for education budgeting across the country, a strategic attempt has also been made to determine the most effective and efficient uses of resources. These efforts have led to such innovations as zero-based budgeting (ZBB), program-planning, and site-based budgeting, which attempt to be more mission-driven and constituent-friendly than traditional types of budgeting in education.

3. Zero-based budgeting (ZBB): Popular in the 1950s and 1960s, ZBB began with the assumption that the school system starts out yearly with a "clean slate" or at a zero spending, with no contents. Thus, each function, program, and agency has to justify its program and its expenditures annually, relating all costs to system goals and objectives to avoid habitual spending.

Hence, budgets are built from the ground up—or from "zero" up. Because many costs, such as tenured teachers' salaries and benefits, are "fixed" across annual budgets, and because the programs are so complex, ZBB becomes more an exercise than a practical reality. As Hartman (1999) explains, "ZBB . . . forces comparisons of and choices among programs and activities that are often difficult to compare adequately" (p. 49).

In addition, most programs are not "up for grabs" on an annual basis, since, for example, schools cannot eliminate their elementary school classes, making such a requirement difficult to justify.

ZBB is not weak in challenging past year's funding but rather strong because it does not just automatically carry over all of prior year costs and spending—when programs or service levels may have changed—and also does not carry over past year's forecasts and assumptions.

ZBB is designed to avoid carrying over priorities and plans as reflected in the budget! While most helpful and sound, ZBB often requires a great deal of time by all key stakeholders. ZBB combined with site-based budgeting (SBB) is perhaps the best approach. SBB tailors the budget more to the unique needs of each school as schools vary by students' needs within districts.

4. Program-planning-budgeting systems (PPBS): Used by the U.S. Defense Department during the Vietnam War, PPBS seeks greater efficiency by attaching spending to particular programs. (For example, the development of a new multipurpose fighter jet aircraft that might be used jointly by the army, navy, and air force—thus saving costs, but failing, in fact, to meet the needs of any of the armed services very well.)

While rarely used in education, PBBS would require school districts to do the following:

(a) Spell out their mission and goals
(b) Lay out alternatives to reach these objectives
(c) Attribute costs to each choice

(d) Analyze the costs
(e) Select the best option
(f) Build the budget around this outcome
(g) Feed data back to adjust the costs-to-the-results

While this method sounds ideal, it often becomes overly complex—and the programs are so numerous that school districts and states cannot readily sustain this approach.

5. Site-based (school-site) budgeting (SBB): SBB is concerned with who will do the budgeting—and where—in the organizational hierarchy that the decisions will be made. In attempts to bring the budgeting process closer to "end-users"—the teachers, students, and school administrators—SBB encourages, if not requires, decision-makers in each school be able to examine their programs and to set their budgets to meet their own particular needs as part of the process of shared decision-making.

Allan Odden et al. (2012) explain that school reform may require greater decentralization, a step "in which teams of individuals—who actually provide the services—are given decision-making authority and held accountable for results" (p. 5). Under SPB, districts must determine the following five steps: (1) who will serve on SBB committees; (2) which decisions and resources are devolved to schools—and using what formulas; (3) how much autonomy is granted to spend for local school needs; (4) exactly how to analyze the budget at each school; and (5) what training and support are needed to make SBB work effectively.

In practice, school districts—or divisions thereof—will utilize variations of many, if not all, of the above methods in compiling their budgets. For example, a school principal may require teachers to justify their individual budget requests (zero-based) in the development of a school (site-based) budget.

A component of the district's budget may include a proposal for a new educational program, including all anticipated expenditures, revenues, and cost savings (program-planning budget). The entire district budget may be shoved into a state-mandated format that requires line items to be categorized by fund, function, program, and object (function/object budgeting).

Outcome-focused budgeting is positive for it relates to outcomes which after all are what education is all about but regarded as too time consuming and complex (few leaders seem to ever wish to agree on outcomes, let alone put them in writing, so they can be held accountable to them). Once the fiscal year begins, the budget is transformed from a financial plan into initial baseline data for a working, dynamic financial accounting system.

How Effective Are the Uses of Funding—and Measured "How"?

The final step, therefore, is to connect *money to results*, outcomes, and student improvements in academic performance. Teachers have no control over whom they teach and what level at which the students are operating when they enter their classrooms in the autumn or spring. Good financial analysis should somehow relate "bucks to outcomes," which is difficult in education

CONCLUSION

The finance officers and staff at the district level are the critical decision-makers and leaders in school district finance. And, likewise, the principals are the "CEO" (chief executive officer) for their schools; therefore, they should know about every classroom, athletic field, closet, hallway, and bathroom. For these are (a) where the supplies and materials are stored; (b) where the teachers are assigned and why they're so assigned—as they are their school community; and, most of all, (c) what are their needs and priorities of their school!

However, per-pupil costs can vary by class/subject, such as high school science (e.g., chemistry labs) can be more expensive than English literature or U.S. history, unless classes travel to the White House to discuss the federal government, meet with President Trump, and understand the needs for governance on-site.

The school-building leaders, thus, need close collaboration and shared information with their school district financial heads and require clear, constant and consistent cooperation, feedback, and help to make their schools work and improve.

Similarly, per-pupil costs can be higher in elementary grades that use manipulatives than in ones that do not; also computer-oriented classes can have higher per-pupil costs for technology-related expenditures. Purchase orders—and the close monitoring of purchasing—are essential to sound budgeting because of the waste and corruption often centers on purchasing: examples are intentional overpaying per unit amounts or receiving less quantity or lower quality but same quantity of items purchased per purchase order!

Business administrators and principals should be aware of how mistakes, even innocent ones, can occur. Close collaboration and sharing information and data are critical to good *fin-man* ("financial management").

Principal leadership is essential to sound budgeting, especially when using site-based budgeting (SBB), indicating that principals have training and instruction in budgeting and school finance to succeed in managing budgets and their schools' operations!

Perhaps one way to reflect on the budget's importance is to consider the following budget impact on the classroom common parlance metric: If they (i.e., meaning key programs, services, technology, materials, furniture, supplies, etc.) are not at our level (i.e., for classroom, school or district), then it won't be in our classrooms for our kids. This is an important guiding principle to keep in mind when budgeting for schools.

Thus, it is recommended to be careful and observant when setting the budget, spending the money, and measuring the results. Money is money and should be used to the teachers' and students' advantages. All educators have financial functions, as they request, receive, and use school district funds. The more the better!

REFERENCES

Bigelow, W. (2016). Nation's largest teachers union endorses teaching "climate justice." *Huffington Post*. Retrieved from http://www.huffingtonpost.com/the-zinn-education-project/nations-largest-teachers_b_11035072.html.

Coffin, S. V., & Cooper, B. S. (Eds.) (2017). *Sound school finance for educational excellence*. Lanham, MD: Rowman & Littlefield.

Cooper, B. S. (1998). Merging the teachers' unions. *Education Week Commentary*, p. 33.

Fusarelli, L. D., & Cooper, B. S. (1999). Why the NEA and AFT sought to merge—and failed. *School Business Affairs, 65*(4), 33–38.

Hartman, W. T. (1999). *School district budgeting*. Reston, VA: Association of School Business Officials International.

Mundt, B., Olsen, R., & Steinberg, H. J. (1982). *Accounting public school budgeting and auditing—Budgeting, accounting, auditing, future trends, managing public resources*. New York: Peat Marwick International.

National School Boards Association (2014). Retrieved from https://www.nsba.org/about-us/frequently-asked-questions#sthash. 9KQci Uyc.dpuf.

Odden, A, & Picus, L. (2012). *School Finance: A Policy Perspective*, Fifth Edition. New York: McGraw Hill.

Thompson, J. (2016). Hillary and the education history that teachers can't forget. *Huffington Post*. Retrieved from http://www.huffingtonpost.com/john-thompson/hillary-and-the-education_b_10868562.html.

White, B. (2016). Fordham Institute, EduWatch.

Chapter 8

Movements to Privatize District Funding in the United States and the United Kingdom

INTRODUCTION

What might happen if the United States, like the United Kingdom, were to begin to "charterize" its public school system, introducing greater family choice, private school ownership, and educational variety—supported by public funding? The British government is now considering the move.

The goal of this chapter is to understand the movement toward private ownership—and public funding—of schools, and thus the notion of "privatization" of education. For as Diane Ravitch (2015) recently reported,

> Last week, addressing his party for the first time since his re-election in May, U.K. Prime Minister David Cameron called for an end to the country's traditional public school system, endorsing instead a nationwide conversion to academies, which are essentially the British equivalent of charter schools—publicly funded, but with greater freedom over what they teach and how they are run. (p. 3)

These "academies" in the United Kingdom would replace the grammar schools, and other public schools, creating a system of government schools that is not only *privately* owned and run but is also *publicly* funded and evaluated. What can the United States learn from and do (or avoid) based on these schools? What are some of the advantages—and disadvantages—of "charterizing," privatizing, and decentralizing the U.S. education system for all. Let's explore some of the advantages first:

1. Increasing Parental Control and Choice: Some have argued that parents need and deserve more choice and control over their own children's education. Already, for generations, parents have often considered the quality

of local schools when selecting where to live, determining which urban neighborhood or which suburb to live in. But once a family settles into a neighborhood, they are likely to be stuck with the local schools, in most cases, whatever their quality—unless they can afford a nearby private school.

For Prime Minister Cameron urged that "current and would-be educators across the U.K.—parents, community groups, social service organizations—to create small new academies known as 'free schools'" (see Cooper, 1971; Ravitch, 2015, p. 1)—"free" as having no tuitions and "free" from total public control.

And the new U.S. education secretary, Betsy DeVos, and President Trump have now discussed a range of privatization programs, including charter schools and private schools.

2. Creating Greater Diversity of Schools: A major private, religious school group in the United States, the Roman Catholics, have seen their schools closing and enrollments dropping—with enrollment peaking in 1965 at 5.66 million students, dropping to under 1.7 million students in 2016—with no end of the decline anywhere in sight.

Perhaps, if some Catholic schools could become *Catholic charter schools* with needed public funding, this move would keep more of Catholic schools and education alive, perhaps without violating the First Amendment by not entangling the "church and the state."

This trend has already started in the United States, with a number of Catholic schools—that were on the verge of closing—becoming charter schools to save themselves. For example, as Eliza Shapiro (2015) reported,

> With Catholic schools closing across New York City and enrollment plummeting 35 percent over the last decade alone, the Queen of Angels and five other Catholic schools in East Harlem and the South Bronx have banded into a "network"—another charter term—of six schools and 2,100 students to try to reverse course.

And the concept has wide appeal to both the United States and United Kingdom, increasing the options, funding, availability, and variety of available schools. Saving Catholic schools is an important step in the educational and religious marketplace in the United States. For as Eliza Shapiro explained,

> the idea is that if these six schools can show substantive improvement over the next several years, the rest of the city's struggling Catholic schools could

follow. And the Partnership's leaders are looking to the city's high-performing charter schools as a template for their revamped schools. (2015, p. 11)

Disadvantages of Publicly Supported Charter Schools:
Private is Private, Independent is Independent: And a Possible Loss of Independence:
What are some of the disadvantages in the U.S.A. of this possible privatization development? In a bureaucracy, even in education, being free from government control has certain advantages, as explained below:

The potential benefits of private schools accrue from their independence. Private schools do not receive tax revenues, so they do not have to follow the same sorts of regulations and bureaucratic processes that govern (and sometimes hinder) public schools. This allows many private schools to be highly specialized, offering differentiated learning, advanced curriculum, or programs geared toward specific religious beliefs. There are exceptions to such generalizations—charter and magnet schools are increasingly common public schools that often have a special educational focus or theme. (Coffin & Cooper, 2017, p. 18)

Further Blurring the Lines: The dangers of moving public and private and religious schools into the same public funding system are numerous, as we run the real possibilities of even a kind of merging of the "Church and State."

Meaning More State Control: And many private schools will likely fear greater public control, which is one reason private schools have long avoided "getting in bed"—so to speak—with the government. As we seek to provide quality education for our children, in public, private, religious schools across the United States, the future is now!

For as Pietras (2015) reminds us historically (if not hysterically):

Our Founding Fathers had seen the cruelty of ecclesiastic courts, forcible tithes and the tyranny of combining church and state. It was a primary reason for Jefferson to say that a "wall of separation" should exist in our country between government and religion. . . . I would remind Andrew Cuomo that he is not the governor of Catholic New York, but the governor of all New Yorkers. (p. 21)

CONCLUSION

The future of the possible steps toward the *charterization* of American nonpublic schools is yet to be determined; perhaps we can learn something from the British, should they likely move in this direction, sooner. Educational leaders, in the United States, should deal with these two questions:

(a) Do schools need private choices to create new programs and improved quality?
(b) What are some of the advantages and disadvantages of "blurring the lines" between public and private school funding, management, and control?

Only the future will answer these questions as we all consider these changes.

REFERENCES

Coffin, S. V., & Cooper, B. S. (Eds.) (2017). *Sound school finance for educational excellence*. Lanham, MD: Rowman & Littlefield.

Cooper, B. S. (1971). *Free and freedom schools: A national survey of alternative programs*. Washington, DC: President's [Nixon's] Commission on School Finance.

Pietras, S. R. (2015, June 28). Funding private schools sets dangerous precedent. *Buffalo New*, p. 21.

Ravitch, D. (2015). Campbell Brown calls for elimination of all public schools. [Blog log post]. Retrieved form https://dianeravitch.net/2015/10/17/campbell-brown-calls-for-elimination-of-all-public-schools/.

Shapiro, E. (2015). Facing decline, Catholic schools form a charter-like network. *PoliticoNew York*. Retrieved from http://www.politico.com/states/new-york/city-hall/story/2015/07/facing-decline-catholic-schools-form-a-charter-like-network-023857.

Chapter 9

Managing School Districts' Funding Programs Now

Quality Education for All

INTRODUCTION

The way forward for better education, now, begins with adequate local school funding, based on careful ways of determining the needs and best uses of school financial resources to carry out a school's mission. This book has pointed the way and given some of the means, methods, and ends to help district financial leadership to make schools financially workable and educationally effective choices and decisions.

This final chapter brings school funding "home," to the school district and the school, where school funding and management are critical and central. For, like other school reforms, quality education depends on quality resources and effective spending, now. Already, organizations are publishing the "goals for the new year, the next year, and the next three to five years." These include the following six steps to reach our goals.

Six Summary Steps for School District Leaders

1. Provide Equity and Opportunity for All Students—Regardless of their Backgrounds, Needs, or Abilities: Recall that education is critical to and for all children, regardless of their background, needs, or income; and overcoming the effects of poverty often depends on the local K–12 school—and the quality of education therein. Education is vital to students, families, society, and our nation. As we discussed in chapter 2,

equitable education means raising enough funding and distributing it equally, effectively, and consistently.
2. Expand Support for Teachers and School Leaders: Money matters and so do effective district and school leaders and teachers. Communities, school boards, and school neighborhoods should seek ways to support and improve their nearby districts and schools, creating a *community of interest* and helping each and every school and classroom and communities for education improvement.
3. Improve Access, Affordability, and Student Outcomes in Postsecondary Education: Now, states are considering making their public colleges and universities tuition-free, as they are currently for the K–12 public schools. While sometimes controversial, especially for private higher education, which charge families thousands of dollars per student, the future may see and need a universal, available, and tuition-free higher and continuing education for all children who qualify and desire a higher education in life. Higher education can mean a fuller life.
4. Promote Greater Use of Evidence and Data: District and school leaders—and their staff—should gather to create, analyze, and use data to keep sight of their goals, problems, and accomplishment. And much of this process will particularly involve district leadership in school finance.

EQUITY FOR ALL

As we discussed in chapter 2 of this book, equitable education means raising enough funding, distributing it equally, effectively, and consistently to all students and schools—and to school districts. As one argument goes:

> Educational equity is dependent on two main factors. The first is *fairness*, which implies that factors specific to one's personal conditions should not interfere with the potential of academic success. The second important factor is *inclusion*, which refers to a comprehensive standard that applies to everyone in a certain education system. These two factors are closely related and are dependent on each other for true academic success of an educational system. (oecd.org)

This book has pointed the way for school districts, teachers, teacher unions, and leaders, to understand the financing of their districts and schools (and classrooms): for example, the funding sources, uses, and importance of dollars for programs, and how to be effective in funding schools. We have reviewed the sources of funding—both public and private—the uses of funds, and the effectiveness in districts and, of course, schools. We review and summarize the quality financial process in this final chapter, in the following steps:

1. Know Funding Sources: Money for education comes from many levels and sources. And district leaders find and track all funds and funding sources, and put them together and raise the money that's available and the leaders' due.
2. Build strong goals and purposes, *with Funding for All*: Keep eyes and ears open and stay alert to program opportunities and other sources of funding.
3. Use Funds Effectively and Equitably: This is so that students and groups are not excluded or underfunded. Make a constant and close attention to see that funds are spent where needed and equitably.
4. Look Public and Private: Money, money everywhere; so check public. Federal, state, and local funding sources—and ways of raising private funding—from local and state and even national organizations.
5. Track Dollars down to the Kids in the Classroom: We have built and patented a system for "tracking dollars to classrooms and kids" (Cooper & Speakman, 2004)—called the Finance Analysis Model (FAM) and *In$ite*—that takes dollars at the system/district level and follows the resources from the "central office" to the classroom, from the superintendents' level to the classrooms to the teachers and their students. FAM is a system for doing the following:

An advanced software package for cost accounting and analysis, management reporting, performance assessment and decision support tool is described. The In$ite™ software package collects, organizes, manages and consolidates financial data and permits the standardized evaluation and comparison of different educational institutions. The software package implements the Finance Analysis Model For Education as a relational database for the efficient and cost-effective management of educational institutions. (Cooper & Speakman, 2004, p. 1)

When first developed in New York City, for Mayor Giuliani in 2003, *In$ite* found that only 21 percent of the enormous district funding actually reached the classrooms, for teachers and kids. So much of these funds were spent on "administration" including the offices, superintendents, and staffing for thirty-one individual "community school boards" in the city. *Driving the bucks to the classrooms and the kids* is essential and involves school funds for teachers, guidance, aides, and other staff; books and materials; and now equipment and computers.

Making Money Matter More in Schools, Now!

Bernard Avishai's diagnoses (2015) of U.S. education are as valid as his prescriptions are naïve. He believes that education can work in all situations for all students. Although he grasps the troubles in our cities, the poor performance of our students, and the need for modernization, Avishai ignores three critical conditions confounding the innovations that he prefers. What is local business's responsibility in educating students in the future?

First, he overlooks the *social context* of schooling. The breakup of family and the breakdown of community, together, adversely affect the ability of children to learn in school and elsewhere.

Second, public schools—fractured, overly specialized, and "loosely coupled" institutions—*are not set up or structured for easy reform*. Try introducing a new computerized mathematics program into a system where teachers work in isolated classrooms, away from other colleagues, and have little or no time to share with and support one another.

And third, public education is a *public monopoly*—and thus has hardly any incentives to innovate at all. Public education was until recently insulated from pressures to compete, change, and improve.

CONCLUSION

Bernard Avishai, and other reformers, should consider many kinds of K–12 schools: public (magnet schools of choice), private, and parochial. Because, as Cooper (1994) argues in the *Harvard Business Review*, we can and should finance our schools, as follows:

1. The major problem is social, not technical. For seventy-five years, critics of schools have concentrated on the *technical* side of the problem: for example, the use of space, time, and technology—and *testing*. In fact, the failure of urban schools mostly results from a breakdown of the social and moral orders, including family, community, church, and school. When 65 percent of the live births in the District of Columbia, for example, are to single, minority mothers under the age of seventeen, the family as we know it has changed. Many of these children from poor, single-parent homes arrive at school ill-prepared.

Avishai seems unaware of the need for *social stability* to make innovations work. How, one wonders, will advanced methods operate in schools, communities, and families that are in chaos? And for some reason, his solutions concentrate almost exclusively on public education, while private and parochial schools seem to work because of their high social capital, strict rules of conduct, and fundamental stability—conditions that are prevalent in traditional homes and communities.

2. School structures resist change. Impoverished, urban school systems are difficult to change because they are such complex, underfunded, and isolated organizations. Pupils and their classes are usually divided by age, grade, ability, needs, subjects, interests, and location, reflecting the ideology of the very bureaucracies that Avishai predicts are vanishing. But, according to Avishai, the modern corporation is being "flattened," opened up, and made free, resembling a small entrepreneurial organization more than a corporate giant.

Mindless work is being performed by "brilliant" computers, freeing humans to do the "zestful" activities associated with new "intelligent enterprises," to use James Brian Quinn's terms. However, while new business enterprises are undergoing a revolution, many schools are not, and their structure is greatly to blame for their inability to change.

3. Public monopolies resist change. Why, one wonders, would public school teachers and administrators even attempt all these radical changes? Adam Smith, of all people, would understand the limits of public monopolies. Without real competition, challenges, and help, agencies have no incentive to change procedures, merge and alter roles, and update, much less eliminate, divisions of labor.

Visits to school classrooms are informative. One sees teachers still keeping students' attendance and performance data in "roll books," not on networked electronic systems. One finds a few old, often useless, computers thrown in a corner and students sitting and staring at teachers—not working and learning at computers. Learning is still too didactic, and sadly not interactive. And students continue to work alone—instead of in groups—around two-way "tele-computers" linked to "spectrum-infinite fiber-networks."

As everyone becomes a lifelong learner, *education*—including its full funding—is indeed critical. But what should business do? It makes little sense, as Adam Smith would warn, to have private corporations invest exclusively in public school monopolies. "It makes little sense," as Adam Smith himself would warn, "to have private corporations invest exclusively in public school monopolies" (Coffin, Cooper, Cattaro, & Howe, 2016, p. 4).

Instead, communities and school district governing boards at the district levels should make a compact involving seeing that public, private, and parochial schools are available for all children, including the inner-city poor. Businesses should extend the compact to help the education of children, not to bankroll more overhead. Innovations that make schools more "thinking," problem-solving, cooperative organizations for children should be expanded.

(3) Communities should concentrate on reforms that improve the structure of individual schools, much as business itself is being reorganized. After all, if public schools themselves are often dull, repetitive, slow-moving places, how can education inspire students, much less help business?

Avishai (2014) is correct that today's learning organizations must become *teaching* organizations and systems. With *business's* help, schools can learn—as they teach as well. Otherwise, we are all in trouble.

And money matters, as improved schools require a smart use of funds, better budgeting, and careful, well-funded and managed school programs. Now, these methods, and this book, provide the background, skills, and methods for school leaders. Use them, as school leaders are most important, critical managers of school funding, budgets, staffing, and programs—and leaders of excellent education of our children, now and in the future.

This book has treated and analyzed the three areas of good district financial management together: (a) funding, (b) leadership, and (c) effective education, as follows.

First, we must know and understand that "money matters" and must be gathered across a wide range of sources and uses. *Good money can mean good resources and quality education.*

Second, *strong district leadership*—for superintendents, school boards, and business officers—is critical. Schools cannot do it alone: they need and depend on the superintendent, school board, and business management to make it work.

Third, we can see how good funding program and policies are a way to bring everything together as *total quality management*: the kids, the teachers, leaders, money, and quality funding programs and policies. Together, these mean good quality leadership, management, and programs.

For as Bonstingl (1992) explains,

> Suddenly, it seems, the name of W. Edwards Deming is everywhere. From relative obscurity in this country a dozen years ago, Deming's name has become synonymous with the movement he calls Quality Management, better known as TQM or Total Quality Management (TQM). This movement is spawning a new American

revolution, as *quality* becomes our watchword in every aspect of life. TQM principles and practices are revitalizing businesses, government agencies, hospitals, social organizations, home life—*and our own world of education.* (p. 22)

We know that money matters in schools and districts—and the wise use of money matters more in the schools for the future education of our children.

REFERENCES

Avishai, B. (April 2, 2012). Real life, not "counter-life". *The Daily Beast.*
Bonstingl, J. J. (1992). The quality revolution in education. *Improving School Quality, 50*(3), 4.
Cooper, B. S. (1994). Educating the workforce of the future and understanding Bernard Avishai. *Harvard Business Review. Special Issue: Developing Employees of the Future.* (Issue authors: Richard Riley, Sandra Feldman, Sofie Sa, Bruce S. Cooper, Diana Wyllie Rigden, Ted Kolderie, Hans Decker, G. Alfred Hess, Jr., and Allyson Tucker), 41–45.
Coffin, S. V., Cooper, B. S., Cattaro, G., & Howe, W. J. (2016). Cristo Rey Schools build social capital for students — and financial stability for schools. Education Next. http://educationnext.org/.
Cooper, B. S., & Speakman, S. T. (2004). The Three R's of Education Finance Reform: Re-Thinking, Re-Tooling, and Re-Evaluating School-Site Information. *Journal of Education Finance, 22*(4), 337–367.

About the Authors

Stephen V. Coffin is a PhD candidate in education at the Graduate School of Education, Rutgers University; he teaches school finance as an adjunct professor at the Graduate Schools of Education for Montclair State University and Rutgers University; teaches school and higher education finance and economics as an adjunct instructor for the Fordham University Graduate School of Education; serves on three editorial review boards; publishes articles, reports, chapters, and books; is a former school business administrator; has earned an MBA in finance and MPA in public administration; and focuses his research on education finance and policy, charter schools, community economic development, school business administration, school choice, and equal educational opportunity and equity.

Bruce S. Cooper, PhD, is professor emeritus of education administration and public policy, Graduate School of Education, Fordham University, New York. He also taught at University of Pennsylvania, University of London, and Dartmouth College, after receiving his doctorate at the University of Chicago with Donald A. Erickson as his mentor. Cooper has written fifty-five books on education politics and policy, including *The Handbook of Education Politics and Policy,* in two editions with Lance D. Fusarelli and James Cibulka. He served as president of the Politics of Education Association (PEA) and is a founding member of Private School Research Association. He received the Jay D. Scribner Award for Mentoring from the UCEA.

www.ingramcontent.com/pod-product-compliance
Lightning Source LLC
Chambersburg PA
CBHW021215240426
43672CB00026B/326